Sugar Flower Skills

Sugar Flower Skills

Alan Dunn

FIREFLY BOOKS

A FIREFLY BOOK

Published by Firefly Books Ltd. 2013

Copyright © 2013 Quarto Inc.

First printing

Publisher Cataloging-in-Publication Data (U.S.)

A CIP record for this title is available from the Library of Congress

Library and Archives Canada Cataloguing in Publication

A CIP record for this title is available from Library and Archives Canada

Published in the United States by
Firefly Books (U.S.) Inc.
P.O. Box 1338, Ellicott Station
Buffalo, New York 14205

Published in Canada by
Firefly Books Ltd.
50 Staples Avenue, Unit 1
Richmond Hill, Ontario L4B 0A7

Color separation in Singapore by Pica Digital Pte Ltd

Printed in China by Hung Hing Printing Group Ltd

Conceived, designed, and produced by
Quarto Publishing plc
The Old Brewery
6 Blundell Street
London N7 9BH

For Quarto:
Project editor: Victoria Lyle
Art editor: Joanna Bettles and Emma Clayton
Designer: Emma Clayton
Photographer: Philip Wilkins
Copyeditor: Corinne Masciocchi
Proofreader: Sarah Hoggett
Indexer: Helen Snaith
U.S. consultant: Dianne Gruenberg
Art director: Caroline Guest
Creative director: Moira Clinch
Publisher: Paul Carslake

Contents

Essential skills — 8

Sugar flower directory — 42

Lily of the Valley — 50

Wild Pansy — 54

Opium Poppy — 88

Flamingo Flower — 92

Hibiscus — 128

Iris — 134

Foreword

My interest in cake decorating and sugarcraft started over 26 years ago, and I have studied almost all aspects of the craft. However, it is the art of making sugar flowers that has fueled my passion and played the biggest part in my approach to cake decorating.

This book is intended as a guide for both the novice and more experienced sugar-flower maker. The Sugar Flower Directory includes some very quick and simple flowers and fantasy forms, as well as more detailed, life-like blooms. I have included a selection of flowers to illustrate the various methods and techniques that can be used to create flowers.

This book also shows how to arrange the flowers and create sprays to display in cake design—the combinations and color schemes are only suggestions and this is an area where you can use your own taste and creative flair to make your work unique to you.

Enjoy yourself and happy flower making!

Alan Dunn

About this book

This book teaches you how to make a stunning selection of sugar flowers. Clear written instructions and step-by-step photographs take you from a ball of gum paste to the finished bloom.

ESSENTIAL SKILLS

This chapter describes the tools and materials used in this book—it tells you what the essential equipment is and how to use each implement to create different effects. The key skills needed to make sugar flowers are also explained in detail with step-by-step photographs.

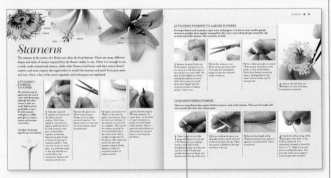

Step-by-step photographs demonstrate key skills.

Do not eat the sugar flowers made in this book. Although gum paste is edible, the presence of wires makes them unsafe to eat.

SUGAR FLOWER DIRECTORY

The directory begins with a beautiful flower selector showing all the flowers in miniature for easy comparison and selection. Once you have chosen the flower you would like to make, turn to the page number indicated, where detailed instructions explain clearly how to make each flower.

The name of the flower and the page number of the relevant instructions are indicated.

Demonstration photographs amplify the written instructions.

The tools and materials required for each flower are listed.

The progress of the flower is pictured at every stage.

A color finder indicates what colors to use and where.

Essential skills

This chapter describes the tools and materials used in this book—it tells you what the essential equipment is and how to use each implement to create different effects. The key skills needed to make sugar flowers are also explained in detail with step-by-step photographs.

Modeling tools

There is a vast array of specialist modeling tools available to help you create almost any effect. However, a set of the essentials is not too expensive, and many tools can be improvised from items already found in your kitchen.

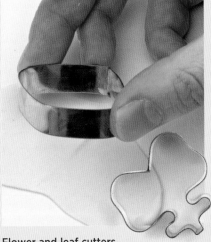

Flower and leaf cutters
There is a huge selection of cutters available from specialist cake decorating stores, the Internet, or by mail order. Available in both metal and plastic, these tools help to speed up the flower-making process and create more consistent results.

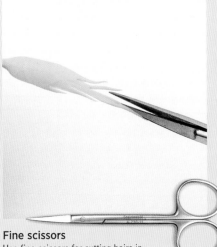

Fine scissors
Use fine scissors for cutting hairs in sepals for roses, snipping the serrated edges of leaves, and texturing buds for various flowers.

Angled tweezers
Look for tweezers without ridges to their grip, as these will leave unattractive "teeth marks" on your flowers. Tweezers are used to pinch ridges on petals and buds, and for inserting stamens into flowers.

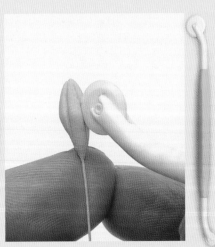

Plain-edge cutting wheel
A plain-edge cutting wheel is great for cutting out petal and leaf shapes and marking central veins.

Star tools
These are ridged tools that are good for dividing pulled flowers into equal proportions.

Nonstick rolling pin
As well as being used to roll out gum paste, the large rounded end can also be used to soften the edges of flowers.

Bone end tool
This tool has a balled, angled end. It is good for creating frilled edges, by pressing against the paste half on the paste and half on your hand or a firm foam pad. It can also be used hollow out cavities.

Ball tools
These come in various sizes in both plastic and metal. They can be used to gently soften the edge of a petal or leaf. To do this, position the tool half on the edge of the petal or leaf and half on your hand or a firm foam pad.

Smooth nonstick modeling tools
These nonstick tools have several uses. The round end can be used in a similar way to a ball tool, while the pointed end is used to open up or indent the center of flowers. It can also be used as a small rolling pin.

Dresden veining tool (broad end)

The broad end of the dresden veining tool can be used to hollow out the center of petals and to work the edges of leaves at intervals to create a slightly serrated or jagged edge.

Dresden veining tool (fine end)

The fine end of the dresden veining tool can be used to create an almost double-frilled effect to the edges of petals—ideal for some orchids. The fine end is used to draw central veins on petals and leaves.

Smooth ceramic tool

This is used as a frilling tool for the edges of petals, giving a frill but without any texture. The pointed end is ideal for opening the throat-like centers of flowers. It can also be used as a small rolling pin.

Ceramic silk veining tool

This very fragile tool can be used to create a delicate, almost silk-like texture to the surface of petals. It can also be used as a frilling tool (see Peony on page 66). Use it against a nonstick board or against your index finger. The rounded end of the tool is also useful for hollowing out the undersides of orchid columns.

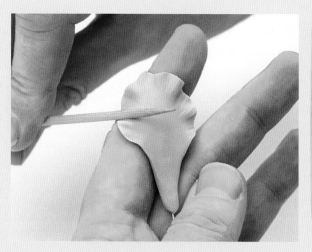

Toothpicks and short wooden skewers
These can be rolled against the edges of petals, leaving a fine vein as well as a frill. Good-quality toothpicks can also be used to add paste color to gum paste.

Petal and leaf veiners
There is a huge selection of commercial, food-grade silicone rubber petal and leaf veiners available to help create natural veining marks.

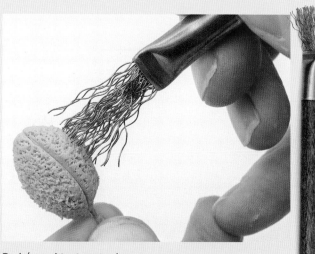

Bark/wood texture tool
A wire brush-type tool is ideal for texturing bark and wood as well as for creating texture for the outer casing of poppy buds.

Corn husk
The dried husk from corn can be very useful as a leaf/petal/bract veiner, where fine straight lines are required, as with bamboo leaves and orchid petals. It is sometimes best to secure the husk to a strong piece of cardstock to hold it in place.

Other useful tools

These tools—from basics, such as paper towel, to more specialist equipment, such as a tape shredder—will all assist the flower making process.

Paper towel
Ideal for many purposes, including making flower formers. To make a flower former, cut a sheet in half diagonally with scissors. Twist the triangular shape back onto itself to form a padded length and then loop and tie the ends into a ring shape. Paper towel is also useful to wrap thin strips around flower stems where a bulkier appearance is needed.

Aluminum foil
This can be used for making formers to dry petals and leaves—it can be manipulated into the required shape and size.

Kettle or clothes steamer
The steam from a just-boiled kettle or a clothes steamer is ideal for setting the color on petals and leaves and takes away the often dry-dusted appearance left by powdered food colors or petal dusts. The steam can also create the waxy or shiny finish required for many types of flowers.

Electric Mixer
A heavy-duty upright electric mixer is indispensable if making your own gum paste.

Measuring spoons (1)
These spoons are essential for measuring small quantities of gum tragacanth, carboxymethylcellulose (CMC), gelatine, white vegetable fat, and liquid glucose used in the gum paste recipe on page 19.

Measuring cups (2)
Measuring cups provide a quick and easy way of measuring confectioner's sugar for gum paste recipes.

Sieve (3)
This common kitchen gadget is essential for getting rid of lumps in confectioner's sugar to create a smooth gum paste.

Corn starch dusting bag (4)
Make a homemade dusting bag from a couple of layers of clean diaper liners filled with a tablespoon of corn starch. Tie together with a length of ribbon or an elastic band. If you can't get hold of diaper liners, use a small square of muslin, the fine casing of a Japanese teabag, or even a clean knee-high.

Nonstick board (5)
A dark nonstick board is easier on the eyes than its white counterpart and also enables you to better judge the thickness of the gum paste.

Nonstick rolling pin (6)
Used for rolling out gum paste. Also see page 11.

Grooved board (7)
This nonstick board has grooves of varying lengths on its surface. You can roll paste over the grooves and cut petals from the paste with ready-made grooves for inserting wires, thus speeding up the process of making wired petals and leaves.

Foam pad (8)
A foam pad can be very useful if you have hot hands. The pad enables you to work the edges of a sugar petal without the heat of your hand causing the paste to stick.

Small palette knife (9)
This is useful for lifting thinly rolled flower paste from a nonstick board as well as for marking indents in the surface of pistils and stamen anthers.

X-acto knife (10)
A sharp X-acto knife is essential for cutting out gum paste petals and leaves.

Scriber (11)
Use a scriber to etch or scratch fine veins onto the surface of colored or glazed leaves and petals to remove lines of color.

Sharp scissors (12)
Small, fine, straight-edged and curved scissors are very useful for working on fine sections of a flower. Larger scissors are good for cutting thread, stamens, and wires.

Wire cutters (13) or strong florist's scissors (14)
Wire cutters are very useful to cut through heavier gauges of wire. Strong florist's scissors are also very useful for this purpose.

Pliers (15)
Needle-nose pliers are used to bend hooks in wires and also help to bend and grip flowers when assembling stems and wiring sprays.

Tape shredder (16)
This very useful piece of equipment cuts florist tape into finer lengths. It contains three razor blades, so care must be taken when using it. The blades can be removed to create half-width tape if needed. It is best to buy two tape shredders: one to cut tape into quarter widths and the other to cut it into half widths. The blades need to be replaced from time to time, as the glue from the florist tape often makes them blunt.

Flower stand and polystyrene dummy cake
Ideal for storing the various flowers and leaves as they are being prepared at their various stages so that they are out of the way but visible and accessible.

For colors and coloring, see pages 28–31.

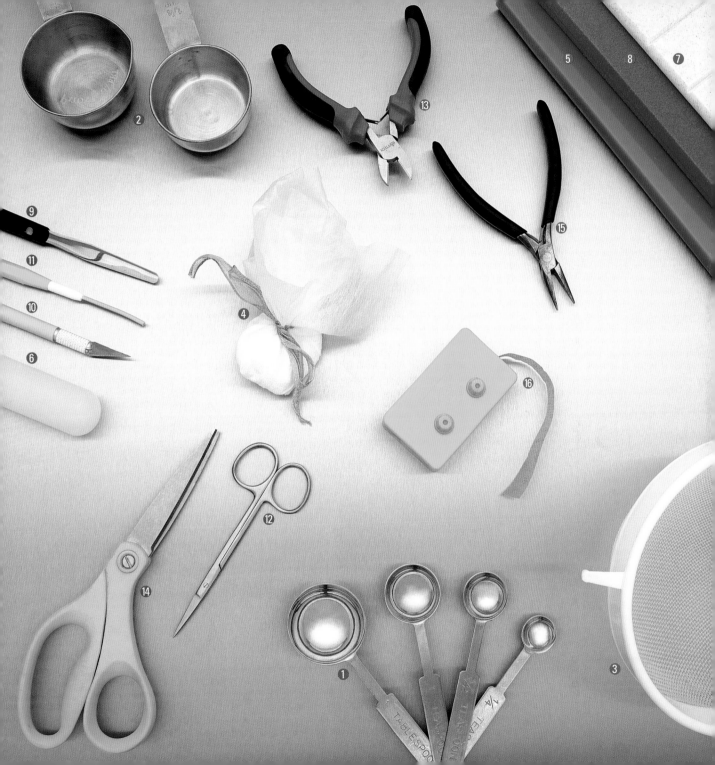

Materials

Listed in this section are the key materials needed to create the flowers in this book. It is always best to source good-quality materials, as this makes the flower-making process both easier and more enjoyable.

Florist tape (1)

This paper tape contains a nontoxic glue that is released when the tape is stretched, making it ideal for creating a fine coating over florist wires and for taping or bonding petals together to form a finished flower shape. Florist tape is available in a range of colors. Some brands of florist tape are already split into half width, although it is often best to buy full-width florist tape and cut it yourself, either by hand or using a tape shredder (see page 14). Keep the rolls of tape wrapped in a plastic bag and in a cool place to prevent the glue from drying out.

Commercial stamens (2)

These are made from paper and sometimes silk. They are inedible and should be used only on items that are not going to be consumed. It is best to buy white or cream stamens and color them as required.

There is a vast range of sizes, styles, and colors.

The more useful stamens for realistic flower-making are the very fine Japanese silk stamens and the miniature (micro) stamens used for smaller flowers.

The most frequently used stamens are the small seed-head stamens. These have a pinched texture to their tips, giving a more realistic effect than the rather dull, round-tipped stamens.

The slightly larger hammerhead stamens and lily stamens are sometimes used, too.

Fine cotton thread (3)

It is important to use cotton thread and not a manmade equivalent, which does not stiffen well with edible gum glue. Threads are available in various gauges—120-gauge lace-making thread is very useful. The tips of the thread may be given a fluffy effect by rubbing the cut ends against an emery board.

Wires

It is best to buy paper-covered wires used specifically for silk, paper, and sugar-flower making. Alternatively, you can buy uncovered florist wires and tape over them yourself with florist tape; however, this is a fairly time-consuming process.

It is best to buy white wires as these have a more general use. They can be colored using dry petal dust or by applying diluted color to a cotton ball disk or nontoxic antibacterial wipe and wiping the color onto the lengths of wire.

Wires also come in nile green and dark green, as well as beige, black, brown, light green, and red. They also come in various gauges— the higher the gauge, the finer the wire. The most commonly used wire gauges are 33, 32, 30, 28, 26, 24, 22, 20, and 18. There are also very fine 35- and 36-gauge wires, as well as some very heavy 16-gauge wire.

Decorative paper-covered wire (4)

These reels of decorative "tourbillon" are available in many colors. This type of wire can be combined with wired sugar flowers to create interesting shapes and lines through floral sprays and arrangements.

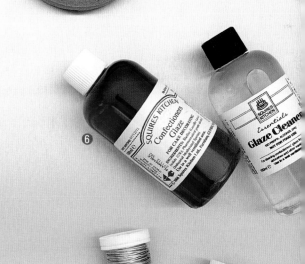

Metallic and fine-crimped wires (5)

These wires are a great addition to floral sprays and arrangements when a little sparkle is needed. They come in different gauges and the color range is vast.

Corn starch

Corn starch is used to prevent gum paste from sticking to tools, veiners, and your hands. Add a tablespoon of corn starch to a homemade dusting bag (see page 14).

White vegetable fat

Use white vegetable fat to lightly grease your nonstick board and then wipe it off with paper towel to ensure that the board is conditioned. This helps to prevent finely rolled gum paste from sticking to the board. Be careful not to use too much fat as this can leave greasy areas on the petals or leaves, causing dark spots in the coloring when petal dusts are applied later. White vegetable fat may also be used to help make gum paste less sticky; however, take care not to add too much,

as this can make a shorter paste and slow down the drying process too much.

Edible gum glue

Edible gum glue may be kneaded into gum paste that is too dry in consistency. It is also used to moisten wires and to stick sugar petals together. You can either buy edible gum glue commercially or create your own by mixing water or clear alcohol with gum paste—care must be taken not to add too much liquid, as this will dissolve the sugar in the gum paste.

Hi-tack nontoxic craft glue

Nontoxic craft glue can be used to bond together inedible stamens and wires to create neat, strong finishes. The glue dries flexible and quite quickly if used sparingly.

Clear alcohol

High-proof alcohols can be mixed with food coloring to add detailed markings to petals and leaves. The alcohol evaporates very

quickly, preventing the sugar from dissolving. Clear alcohol is also used with confectionery glaze to make glazes.

Confectionery glaze (6)

This solution is made from a mixture of high-proof alcohol and food-grade shellac, often used as a coating for pills. It may be applied to petals and leaves using a paintbrush, although this often creates a streaky effect and tends to damage the bristles of the brush, so it is preferable to dip the item into the glaze and then shake off the excess. Used neat, the glaze gives a very shiny finish; for less of a shine, dilute it with clear alcohol (see page 33).

Edible glaze spray

These spray varnishes are a mixture of food-grade shellac and clear alcohol in a pressurized spray form. They are used to glaze gum paste. Some spray varnishes can be very shiny and should be used carefully. Some brands dry quickly while others take longer to dry (see page 33).

Gum paste

Gum paste is a soft, malleable paste that sets very firmly when left to dry in air. It is perfect for making sugar flowers because it holds its shape well, so it can be rolled out very thinly to make delicate petals or leaves. It is not sticky, so it works well with molds and veiners. Gum paste is available in various colors, although you can color the basic white and cream varieties yourself.

ALL ABOUT GUM PASTE

Cane sugar came from Polynesia and gradually made its way through to India. In 510 BC the Emperor Darius of Persia invaded India, where he found the plant described as "the reed which gives honey without bees" which he then introduced into the Middle East. Coincidently, the plant that gives gum tragacanth is native to the Middle East, too; it has many uses, including a herbal medicine and a traditional binder for pastels and incense sticks. So it seems that it was inevitable that the two ingredients should be combined together at some stage.

It was the Crusaders in the 11th century who first introduced sugar to Western Europe. It is unclear as to who would have made the very first wired sugar flowers, although the traditional art of Japanese flower-making was being practiced about 500 years ago using a paste made from sugar, white beans, and rice flour with the combination of natural traditional Japanese food dyes. In England around the same time, the Tudors were using a gum paste/pastillage to create plates, goblets, and table centerpieces as well as decorative unwired leaves and basic flowers for the court of Henry VIII. During the late 19th century, the Victorians adorned their rather grand cakes with wired sugar flowers. Sadly, the art died out during the World Wars because of sugar rationing, although it continued in the Colonies.

STORING

Gum paste is an air-drying paste, so it is important to keep it double-wrapped in food-grade plastic and in an airtight container in the fridge. The paste may also be frozen if it is packed into an airtight container. When you need it, simply defrost the paste, remove it from the bag, re-knead it, and place it in a fresh plastic bag.

GUM PASTE RECIPE

There are many brands of gum paste available commercially throughout the world, with variations in consistency, drying times, and strength. It is often preferable to find a brand that works for you, as commercially made gum pastes are often more consistent to work with than homemade ones. However, if you prefer to make your own (if you cannot find ready-made gum paste or if the ready-made gum paste available is very expensive), this recipe makes a good, pliable, and strong paste.

Ingredients

Makes roughly 1 lb (500 g) gum paste

- 5 tsp (25 ml) cold water
- 2 tsp (10 ml) unflavored gelatine
- 1 lb/3 cups (500 g) confectioner's sugar
- 3 tsp (15 ml) gum tragacanth or 5 tsp (25 ml) carboxymethylcellulose (CMC)
- 1 tsp (5 ml) of cream of tartar (optional) (helps the gum paste to dry in humid conditions)
- 2 tsp (10 ml) liquid glucose
- 3 tsp (15 ml) white vegetable fat, plus 1 tsp (5 ml) extra for later
- 1 large fresh egg white

1 In a small bowl, mix together the cold water and powdered gelatine and leave to stand for 30 minutes. Meanwhile, sift the confectioner's sugar and gum tragacanth or carboxymethylcellulose together (and the cream of tartar, if using) into the bowl of a heavy-duty food mixer.

2 Next, place the bowl with the now spongy gelatine mixture over a small saucepan of hot water and stir until it has dissolved. Warm a measuring teaspoon in hot water, measure out the liquid glucose, and add it to the gelatine mixture—the heat of the spoon helps to ease the glucose on its way. Now add 3 teaspoons (15 ml) of the white vegetable fat and blend into the mixture. Continue to heat the mixture until everything has dissolved.

3 Pour the dissolved mixture into the confectioner's sugar/gum tragacanth mixture and add the fresh egg white. Set the mixer to its lowest speed to mix the ingredients together. Gradually increase the speed to maximum until the paste is white and stringy.

4 Remove the paste from the bowl, place it on a clean nonstick board, and knead it into a smooth ball. Smear the ball of gum paste evenly and lightly with the remaining teaspoon of white vegetable fat. This coating helps to prevent the outer surface of the paste from forming a dry crust that potentially can leave hard, gritty bits in the paste at the rolling-out stage. Place the paste in a plastic food bag and store in an airtight container. Although the paste may be used once cooled, it is often best to allow it to rest and mature for 12 hours before using.

WORKING WITH GUM PASTE

PREPARING THE BOARD

Before working with gum paste, lightly grease a nonstick board with white vegetable fat, then wipe it off using dry paper towel. This keeps the board conditioned and helps release thinly rolled gum paste from the board. You will need to keep reapplying the white fat from time to time, otherwise the gum paste will stick to the board. Greasing the board also removes any unwanted petal dust color that may be lurking.

PREPARING THE PASTE

Break off a small piece of paste. It will be quite firm and sometimes a little crumbly. Knead it between your fingers and thumbs to warm it up and manipulate the gums in the paste to make it more pliable, stretchy, and malleable. Do not use any corn starch at this stage. The paste will start to make a clicking sound in your fingers as it is being kneaded—this is a sign that it is ready to use.

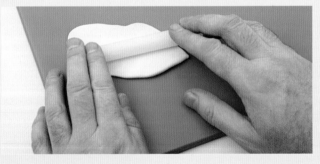

GETTING THE RIGHT CONSISTENCY

If the paste feels too dry, simply knead a little edible gum glue into it; if it feels too sticky, add a tiny amount of white vegetable fat—but be careful not to add too much, as this will result in a "shorter" paste and will slow down the drying process. Wrap the paste in a plastic bag when not in use.

ROLLING

Take the required amount of well-kneaded gum paste. Using a nonstick rolling pin, roll it out onto a lightly greased and cleaned-off nonstick board. It is wise not to roll a large quantity of paste, as this can be hard work and the paste will dry out. Keep rolling the paste until it is the required thickness. Use a small palette knife to help lift and peel the paste off the board. At this stage, the side of the paste that has been against the board tends to be a little sticky—turn the paste over to breathe, dust it very lightly with corn starch, and then cut out the petal or leaf shapes.

BASIC TECHNIQUES

Once your gum paste is ready to work, you can use your hands to model basic shapes or use the modeling tools to perform some of these core techniques.

Making a ball
Work a piece of gum paste until it is pliable. Place it in the palm of your hand and firmly rotate it with your forefinger, gradually decreasing the pressure to form a round ball.

Making a teardrop shape
Make a ball of paste (see left). Roll your forefinger backward and forward over half the ball, applying pressure to form the paste into a cone or, with more pressure, a tapered cone shape.

Making a hat shape
Make a cone shape (see left). Pinch the broad end of the shape between your fingers and thumb to create a hat shape. Continue to pinch the brim of the hat to thin it out slightly.

Pinching
Hold the petal between your thumb and index finger. Carefully but firmly pinch from the base of the petal toward the tip to both emphasize the central vein and curl the tip. You might need to stretch the petal a little as you curl it to create a tight curl at the tip.

Softening
Place the petal on a firm foam pad or the palm of your hand. Using the ball tool, gently work the gum paste half on the petal and half on your pad/hand to thin the edge and give a little movement.

Ruffling
Place the petal on a firm foam pad or the palm of your hand. Using the ball tool, with a little pressure work the gum paste half on the petal and half on your pad/hand to create a ruffled edge on the petal.

Frilling
Place the petal against your index finger or the nonstick board and use a short wooden skewer or silk veining ceramic tool to work the edge at intervals—this will thin the edge and create a frill, too. Keep the point of the tool up and don't dig it into the petal.

Using cutters

Although flowers and foliage can be made without cutters, using them does speed up the flower-making process and also helps to create more consistent results.

There are hundreds of different types of petal, flower, and leaf cutters commercially available made from plastic, metal, and occasionally from various resins. It can often be a daunting task knowing which ones to buy. Some cutter shapes can be used for more than one flower and some metal cutters can be squashed slightly, making them suitable for other types of flowers and leaves, so it is advisable to buy two sets of the more useful shapes. For leaves with serrated or fine sections, choose a plastic cutter as metal cutters with serrated edges often create a more stylized effect.

CUTTING A PETAL/LEAF THAT IS TO BE WIRED

1 Lightly grease a nonstick board with white vegetable fat and then wipe it off with dry paper towel. You will need to keep reapplying white fat from time to time, otherwise the paste will stick to the board, especially if it is very fine.

2 Form a ball of well-kneaded gum paste into a long teardrop shape. Place the shape against the nonstick board and flatten it using the side of your hand.

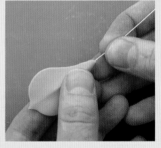

3 Thin out the paste using a small nonstick rolling pin or dowel, leaving a thick ridge down the center. Keep rolling the paste on either side of the ridge. Start to roll the pin/dowel at a slight angle on either side of the ridge to create a tapered ridge shape.

4 Lift the paste from the board and move it to an area of the board that is lightly dusted with corn starch. Place the cutter on the paste so that the thick ridge lines up with the center of the length of the cutter. Press the cutter firmly against the paste and board to cut out the shape. Sometimes, a gentle scrubbing action with the cutter creates a cleaner cut edge.

5 Pick up the cutter with the paste still attached to it and use your thumb to rub the paste against the edge of the cutter—this takes away the slightly untidy edge. Release the paste from the cutter.

6 Next, moisten the end of the wire with edible gum glue and carefully insert it into the thick ridge of the shape. Support the ridge with your finger and thumb as you gradually insert the wire—this will help guide the wire and hopefully prevent it from piercing through the paste. The wire should be inserted about one-third to half the length of the shape to give it support.

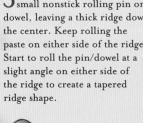

Cleaning cutters

Although most metal cutters are stainless steel, it is advisable not to get them wet. Instead, use a new, dry toothbrush to clean off any excess pieces of dried gum paste left behind during the flower-making process.

CUTTING OUT A HAT-SHAPED FLOWER

1 Form a ball of well-kneaded gum paste and then apply pressure with your index finger to one side of the ball to work it into a cone shape. You might need a little corn starch if the paste feels sticky.

2 Continue to work the paste against the palm of your hand or a nonstick board to create an elongated cone/teardrop shape. Next, smooth the long section to create a more elegant, slender-neck shape.

3 Use your fingers and thumbs to pinch out the base of the shape to form a "hat" shape. Continue to pinch the rim of the hat to thin it out slightly. Keep pinching around the base of the central neck to create a finer area—this will make it easier to slide the flower cutter over the neck of the flower.

4 Place the shape back against the nonstick board, with the "brim" of the hat flat against the board. Use a dowel or nonstick modeling tool to roll out the brim to thin it evenly. Lift up the shape and place it on an area of the board that has been lightly dusted with corn starch.

5 Carefully place the cutter over the neck of the flower and press it firmly against the rolled-out paste. Quickly cut out the shape, gently scrubbing the cutter against the board to encourage the shape to remain in the cutter.

6 Next, pick up the cutter with the flower still in it. Rub your thumb over the edge of the cutter to create a clean-cut edge and remove any ragged edges.

7 Use the pointed end of a dowel or modeling tool to push from the cut, flat side of the flower to release the shape from the cutter. Open up the center of the shape with the pointed end of the modeling tool, work the petals or leaves as required, and then thread a hooked wire through the center.

Templates

Although there are many cutters available commercially to make leaves and petals, it is sometimes necessary to make pieces using templates.

Keep a record of the various flowers and leaves you see as inspiration and reference material for the next time you are required to make a flower. Dissecting a flower and drawing around the petal shapes and leaves is a good way of creating very accurate work. Use watercolor paints, colored pencils, or aqua crayons to add color and markings to your drawings. Alternatively, you could take photographs. Include shots of the various parts of the plant as well as close-ups of petals and leaves. Place a ruler in the same shot so that you have a record of the scale. Or you could photocopy the various parts of the flower to record the exact size, shape, and coloring. All these can be used as the basis for a template.

Materials

- Paper
- Tracing paper
- Cardstock or plastic

Equipment

- Pencils
- Watercolor paints, colored pencils, or aqua-crayons
- Camera
- Photocopier
- Scanner (optional)
- Sharp scissors
- X-acto knife
- Plain-edge cutting wheel

All the templates for the flowers in the book can be found on pages 168–173.

MAKING AND USING A TEMPLATE

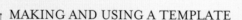

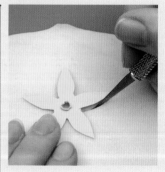

1 Trace the template onto cardstock or plastic (for example, ice-cream or margarine containers) and cut the shape out using sharp scissors.

2 For hat-shaped flowers, you will need to cut a hole at the center of the blossom shape to fit over the central node.

3 Roll out some gum paste to the desired thickness and place the cut-out template on top. Cut around the shape using a sharp X-acto knife or plain-edge cutting wheel.

Making veiners

There are hundreds of commercially produced petal and leaf double-sided veiners on the market, although sometimes you might need to make your own molds or veiners from a real leaf or petal.

There are many mold-making kits on the market, but it is important that you find one that is nontoxic and safe to use with food items. There are two compounds in the kit: one is blue (the catalyst) and the other is white (the base). Once you have mixed the two compounds together you have to work quite fast, as it only takes about 10–20 minutes before the mixed media set. The silicone putty tends to stick to surfaces, so handle the paste on a food-grade plastic bag.

Materials

- Silicone putty
- Fresh leaf or petal
- Facial cold cream cleanser

Equipment

- Nonstick board
- Food-grade plastic bags
- Measuring spoons
- Sharp scissors
- X-acto knife or scriber

1 Use separate measuring spoons to scoop equal amounts of the blue and white compounds to avoid "setting" areas on the remaining compounds. Mix the two compounds together thoroughly, but try not to knead in too many air bubbles.

2 Press the silicone putty onto a food-grade plastic bag and then press the back of the petal or leaf into it, taking care to press the surface evenly to avoid air bubbles, which will create a fault in the finished veiner. Leave to set until firm.

3 When the putty has set, peel off the leaf or petal. Use sharp scissors to trim away any excess from around the edge of the mold. Often, the veining on the top half of a leaf or petal is slightly different from the back, so you might decide to leave the leaf or petal in the first half of the veiner to take a cast of the upper surface. I prefer to use the side with the strongest veining.

4 To create the second half of the veiner, lightly grease the leaf or petal veiner with cold cream cleanser. Be careful not to use too much, as this will clog up the finer veins and may also cause air bubbles in the veiner.

5 Mix the two compounds as before and press on top of the first part of the veiner. Sometimes it is best to add small amounts to very detailed areas and then build the compound up to form the whole veiner. Press the compound evenly to pick up the details. Leave to set as before and then carefully pry the two sections apart.

Color theory

The coloring process is a vital part of flower-making and cake decorating. It can often be quite a daunting task trying to figure out color combinations. You can always look to nature to see which colors work best together, although often you will be surprised just how stunning a bunch of clashing colored flowers look.

Inspiration for color
Most of the time you will be using the real colors of nature, above, for your sugar flowers.

COLOR WHEEL

Understanding the principles behind an artist's color wheel can help give you confidence when choosing colors for your displays. Once you understand a few color rules, you can use them to achieve particular effects.

Remember, a color wheel is based on true pigment color and food colors are not always an exact pigment. For instance, many of the blue food colors can be a little dull. Even so, it is still often a good idea to consult the color wheel for a little guidance or inspiration.

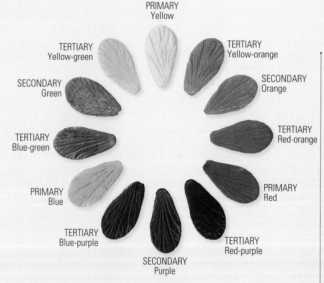

PRIMARY
Yellow

TERTIARY
Yellow-green

TERTIARY
Yellow-orange

SECONDARY
Green

SECONDARY
Orange

TERTIARY
Blue-green

TERTIARY
Red-orange

PRIMARY
Blue

PRIMARY
Red

TERTIARY
Blue-purple

TERTIARY
Red-purple

SECONDARY
Purple

Primary, secondary and tertiary colors

Red, yellow, and blue are the three primary colors from which every other color is made. Mix any two primary colors together to create orange, green, and violet—these are known as secondary colors. Mix together a primary and a secondary color and you create a tertiary color.

Complementary colors

Complementary colors are colors that sit opposite each other on the color wheel and are said to complement each other. So for instance, red is complementary to green, orange is complementary to blue, and yellow is complementary to violet.

Tints and shades

A tint is a color mixed with white. A shade is a color mixed with black. Tints are useful for creating delicate pastel colors for flowers. The lightness or darkness of a color is described as its value.

Harmonioius or analogous colors

These are colors that sit next to each other on the color wheel—for example, yellow, green, and blue or yellow, orange, and red.

COLOR SCHEMES

You can use color theory to help you put together different-colored flowers in beautiful sprays. Of course, these are just a few of many starting-off points; the key is experimentation and judging by eye what looks good.

Monochromatic

Monochromatic sprays are deceptively simple, yet can be very striking. In order to create visual interest, use flowers of different sizes and textures. For example, here the large petals of the gardenia balance the small buds of the lily of the valley.

Harmonious

Using harmonious flowers creates colorful but unified displays. Where on the color wheel you choose your colors from will influence the effect you create: yellows, oranges, will create bright, warm sprays; purples, blues, and greens, will create cool, sophisticated sprays. It is best not to use all the colors at full strength as this can create a gaudy result.

Pastel colors

Flowers in pastel colors look very pretty together. Using flowers in pastel colors also enables you to use colors together that might otherwise clash with one another. Mix the colors lighter, but still follow the natural color-value variation within the flower.

Contrasting/complementary

Complementary-colored flowers provide a strong visual contrast and produce interesting, eye-catching schemes. It is often best not to use equal quantities of complementary-colored flowers in a spray (as it can create a clashing effect)— instead, let a few flowers "pop" against contrasting foliage.

Types of color

There are hundreds of pastes and petal dusts available commercially, making it easy for the flower-maker or sugarcrafter to produce effective flowers. Sometimes, however, you will need to mix your own colors to achieve the effect you require.

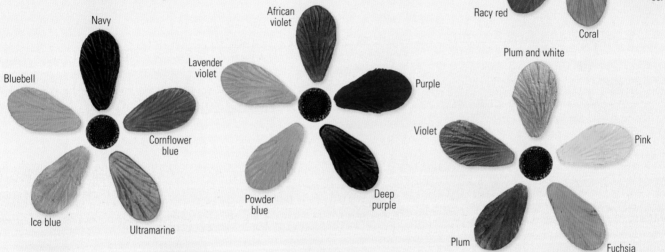

Kiko
Ruby
Nasturtium
Red
Eggplant
Racy red
Coral

Navy
African violet
Lavender violet
Purple
Bluebell
Plum and white
Cornflower blue
Violet
Pink
Powder blue
Deep purple
Ice blue
Ultramarine
Plum
Fuchsia

Paste food colors
These often glycerol-based concentrated food colorings are ideal for coloring gum paste without altering the consistency too much. Paste colors may also be diluted with water or clear alcohol so that they can be used as a painting medium.

Liquid colors
Liquid food colors are used as a painting medium to add detail spots or stripes and markings on petals and leaves. They are not often used to color gum paste as they tend to alter the consistency of the paste, making it too sticky, especially if strong colors are added.

Petal dusts
Petal dusts are mostly used dry, dusted onto the surface of petals and leaves to create realistic, often very vibrant effects. White petal dust may be added to colors to tone them down a little. These dusts contain edible gums that help them to adhere to the surface of the paste. Petal dusts can also be diluted with clear alcohol and used as a painting medium for more solid effects and for finer detail markings (see page 31). The colors may also be kneaded into gum paste to create subtle coloring (see page 30).

Craft dusts
Craft dusts are nontoxic but nonedible. They can be used on wired flowers that are removed from the cake prior to eating and when the flowers will not be consumed. They mostly include the very bright pinks, blues, and purples.

Petal dusts used

The petals on these two pages show the petal dusts used in the book and demonstrate the wonderful selection of colors available. Please note that the colors are subject to printing limitations.

Nutkin brown

Moss green

Forest green

Vine green

Brown

Holly green

Black

White

Sunflower

Daffodil

Champagne

Foliage green

Cactus

Bluegrass

Woodland green

Egg yellow

Skintone

Tangerine

Terracotta

PAINTBRUSHES AND FOOD COLOR PENS

Use good-quality paintbrushes for both dusting dry colors and painting finer details. Synthetic fiber brushes are best for applying petal dusts, as the scrubbing action often required to create strong coloring can make the tips of a sable brush fuzzy. The bristles of the brush should be both soft and firm and not too long. Try to keep brushes separate for different colors—a few for yellow, green, blue, red, etc. If you do need to clean the color from a brush, simply brush it through with corn starch. Brushes can be washed with baby shampoo. Buy a selection of sizes so that you always have the right brush for the work you are creating.

Flat and filbert

Flat and filbert brushes are best for creating intense coloring.

Sable or synthetic brushes

For fine detail painting, sable or synthetic brushes work well.

Food color pens

These pens contain food coloring and are useful for adding small spots and detail markings to flowers and foliage.

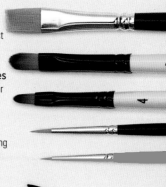

Luster petal dusts

These shimmering dusts are great to use if a softer, delicate, almost silk-like flower effect is required. The colors may be used dry or diluted with clear alcohol to create a painting medium to add detail veining and spots to flowers and leaves, as with begonia and cyclamen leaves.

Pollen dusts

Some of these commercially available pollen dusts are made from a mixture of semolina (or similar) and food color, while others are made from fine sugar and color. Of course, you can also make your own, combining semolina with powder food color to create various degrees of texture. Pollen can be attached to stamens using a little fresh egg white.

Nontoxic craft glitter

These glitters are not edible and should not be used on anything that is to be consumed. However, they may be used sparingly on non-edible items, such as wired sugar flowers, that will be removed from the cake prior to eating.

Applying color

You can apply liquid, paste, and powder color in different ways to create a variety of effects, from kneading it into gum paste to adding detail.

Ways of mixing
You can either add small amounts of color at a time until your reach your desired color. Or you can color a small amount of gum paste to a good depth, then take small amounts of the colored paste and add it to a larger amount of white gum paste.

MIXING GUM PASTE WITH PASTE COLORS

If you need to color large amounts of gum paste, then use liquid or paste colors. Some colors tend be become stronger than first intended, so let the paste rest for a while before making the flower. This gives you a chance to add more white paste if the color is too strong.

1 Take a clean toothpick, dip the end into the paste food color, and add this color to your paste.

2 Knead the paste to blend the color evenly.

MIXING GUM PASTE WITH POWDER COLORS

You can only color small quantities of gum paste to create pale colors with petal dusts, as adding too much powder will dry out the paste (although you can soften the paste by adding a little edible gum glue).

1 Use a clean, small palette knife to place the petal dust color on the gum paste.

2 Knead the paste to blend the color evenly.

CREATING DEPTH WITH PETAL DUST

It is often best to dust sugar petals and leaves with petal dusts before the gum paste has a chance to dry, so that the petal dusts adhere easily to the surface of the paste to create intense coloring and depth. The dusts contain gums that help them to stick to the paste—but if you dust a completely dry petal or leaf, you have to scrub the color onto the paste much harder and you run the risk of breaking or damaging the piece.

PETAL DUST PAINT

Diluting petal dusts with clear alcohol creates a paint that may be used as a base coat to create a more intense coloring or to add detail.

Depth can created by applying petal dust heavily at the base of the petal, using a flat dusting brush. Gradually fade the color toward the center and edges of the petal.

Depth can be added to the center of a flower to create a stronger-colored focal area. Here, a rose is being dusted intensely at the center to create a bold effect.

Use petal dusts in layers to create an interesting effect and more depth to your work. Here, the petal is dusted intensely with orange petal dust and then overdusted with red petal dust.

Liquid food colors or diluted paste or powder colors may also be used to paint fine detail spots and markings onto petals and leaves.

COLORING LEAVES

Leaves are not just colored green! Catching the edges with a contrast color and layering in different shades can bring them to life and make your sprays look all the more realistic.

1 Catching the edge of a leaf with red or eggplant petal dust helps to add a little detail. Sometimes it helps to introduce a little of the flower color into the leaf, too.

2 Use layers of green petal dust to create realistic foliage effects and more depth. Here, forest green is dusted lightly from the base of the leaf, fading toward the edges.

3 Overdust with lighter greens, blending them together and scrubbing the color into the surface of the leaf. The front of a leaf is nearly always darker than the back. Shake off the excess color.

4 Drag a flat brush loaded with color against the raised veins on the back of a petal or leaf to emphasize them with color. Shake off the excess color.

Steaming & glazing

The use of petal dusts on flowers and leaves often leaves quite a dry, dusty finish and sometimes the colors can drift onto the surface of the cake. To counteract this, and to give flowers, leaves, and fruit a more natural finish, either steam or glaze your flowers. White vegetable fat and oil sprays may also be used for glazing purposes; however, they have a tendency to attract dust.

Before

STEAMING

Steaming flowers and leaves helps "set" the petal dust color and leaves a gentle sheen. It can also create a waxy effect, suitable for the petals of flowers such as orchids, gardenias, and stephanotis.

1 Hold the sugar flower over the steam from a just-boiled kettle, taking extreme care not to scald yourself. Alternatively, you might prefer to use the steam from a clothes steamer. Take care not to steam too heavily, as this can create a very plastic effect and also dissolve some of the flower. Leave the flower to dry before using it on a cake.

2 The steaming process is also useful if you need to add more depth to a flower or create an almost velvety effect, as with red roses. Dust the flower as required, steam, and allow the moisture to dry a little before re-dusting with more petal dust.

After

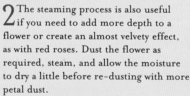

CONFECTIONERY VARNISH

Confectionery varnish, diluted with clear alcohol if necessary (see "Mixing your own glaze" below), creates a more natural, stronger shine than steaming. Take care not to get the glaze onto work surfaces, as it is difficult to remove once dried.

Use confectionery varnish neat or dilute it with clear alcohol. Quickly dip the leaf, petal, or berry into the glaze and then remove and shake off the excess glaze. You might need to re-dip some items where a heavy shine is needed, for berries or shiny foliage, for example. Set aside to dry before using the item in a spray or arrangement.

Confectionery varnish may also be painted onto the surface of the item—but take care, as often streaks will form with the layers of petal dust. Some people prefer to steam the item first, leave it to dry, and then paint or dip it into the glaze. However, this often traps too much moisture in the sugar, creating a very weak/fragile finished piece.

Edible glaze spray

Edible glaze spray is a glaze conveniently ready mixed in an easy-to-use spray can. You must work in a well-ventilated area when using it and wear a mask if you are glazing lots of items. Spray the item very lightly, using quick and short bursts, then leave to dry. Spray again if a shinier effect is required. Take care not to get any spray onto furniture, work surfaces, or eyeglasses, as it is very difficult to remove. It is best to spray into a cardboard box to control the excess glaze.

ETCHING

Once the glaze has dried, you can add veins by etching into the surface of the leaf.

Allow the glazed item to dry. Use a scriber or X-acto knife to scratch or etch through the glaze, layer of petal dust, and part of the sugar, to create fine, delicate, pale veining.

MIXING YOUR OWN GLAZE

Create your own glaze by mixing confectionery varnish and clear alcohol in a clean preserves jar. Screw on the lid and shake gently to create an even mixture. You will need to shake the mixture from time to time to avoid separation. The following combinations are the most useful:

QUARTER-GLAZE
Use three-quarters clear alcohol to one-quarter confectionery varnish. This is used for leaves that do not need much shine. It is a good mixture to take away the very flat, dusty look left by petal dust on a petal or leaf.

HALF-GLAZE
Use equal proportions of clear alcohol and confectionery varnish. This is the most useful glaze and is used for many leaves, including rose, peony and ivy leaves.

THREE-QUARTER GLAZE
Use one-quarter clear alcohol to three-quarters confectionery varnish. This gives a demi-gloss without leaving a "plastic" effect. Useful for some berries, ruscus foliage, and holly leaves.

Stamen
Stigma
Pistil
Stamen
Pistil
Stamen

Stamens

The stamens at the center of a flower are often the focal feature. There are many different shapes and styles of stamen required for the flower-maker to use. Often it is enough to use a ready-made commercial stamen, while other flowers look better with fine cotton thread centers, and some require the sugarcrafter to model the stamens and pistil from gum paste and wire. Here, a few of the more regularly used techniques are explained.

ATTACHING STAMENS TO A WIRE

The stamens may be taped onto the end of a wire with florist tape, although this often creates a little too much bulk and it is preferable to use a hi-tack nontoxic craft glue or edible gum glue to create a neater and stronger connection.

The Babies' Bonnet (see page 80) uses wired stamens.

1 Take the required number of stamens for the flower you are making. Hold them tightly at one end and apply a small amount of hi-tack nontoxic craft glue to bond them together at the base. Squeeze the glue firmly to secure the group of stamens together. Take care not to use too much glue, as it will take longer to dry and will add too much bulk to the connection between the stamens and the wire.

2 Leave the glue to set for a few minutes (longer if it is a larger group of stamens). Use sharp scissors to trim away the excess stamen tips at the glued end.

3 Apply a tiny amount of glue to the end of a paper-covered wire. Press the wire onto the base of the stamens to secure the two together. Next, pinch the stamens around the wire and hold firmly to the count of 10—this is usually enough time for the glue to take a grip and secure the wire and stamens together firmly. Repeat to make the required number of stamen centers.

4 Some flowers require curved stamens. To create these, use the blade of a pair of scissors to gently curve the length of the stamens. Dust or paint the tips and base of each stamen as required prior to inserting into the flower.

ATTACHING STAMENS TO LARGER FLOWERS

For larger flowers such as peonies, open roses, and poppies, it is best to create smaller groups of stamens and glue them together starting from the center and working the glue toward the tips on both ends of the stamens. This cuts down on bulk.

1 Squeeze the glue firmly into the stamen, trying not to use too much as it will take longer to dry and give too much bulk. The glue shrinks slightly as it dries, causing the stamens to twist a little—don't worry too much about this. Repeat with the required number of stamen groups. Leave to set.

2 Use fine scissors to cut the stamen groups in half. Trim away the excess glued length to leave the required length of stamen.

3 Use a little more glue to attach the groups of stamens to the pistil or ovary of the flower. Pinch them firmly around the center, holding them to the count of 10 to create a good strong bond.

4 Leave to dry and then use tweezers to curve and shape the stamens as required.

GUM PASTE WIRED STAMENS

There are many flowers that require fleshier stamens, such as lily stamens. These are best made with wire covered with a fine layer of gum paste.

  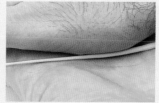 

1 Take a length of wire (the gauge will depend on the size of the flower you are making). Attach a small ball of well-kneaded gum paste onto the wire and then work it firmly and quickly between your finger and thumb toward the tip of the wire.

2 Keep working the paste—you might need to pinch off some of the excess from the tip. Often the stamen is fleshier at the base and finer at the tip.

3 Smooth the length of the stamen between your palms or against a nonstick board. Curve as required.

4 Attach the anther using edible gum glue, then leave to dry. Color as required. It is sometimes necessary to bend the wire in a "T" shape at one end prior to adding the paste. This gives the anther more support and strength when attached.

COTTON THREAD STAMENS

Some flowers have many very fine stamens at their center and it is often best and also cheaper to use fine cotton thread to create these. It is important to use cotton thread, as nylon threads tend not to respond well to being stiffened with edible gum glue. There are various gauges of thread—120-gauge used by lacemakers is very useful for many small to medium flowers.

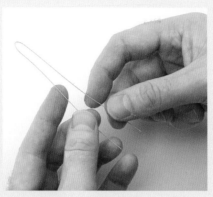

1 Bend a length of wire in half (the gauge will depend on the size of the flower you are making).

2 Wrap some fine cotton thread several times around two parted fingers to form a large loop. Remove the loop from your fingers and twist it into a figure-eight shape. Next, fold the shape in half to form a smaller, bulkier loop.

The Thistle (see page 70) uses cotton thread "stamens" to represent the plume.

3 Thread the prepared wire through the center of the loop and tape the base of the thread down onto the wire using quarter-width florist tape.

4 Bend and twist another wire and insert it into the opposite side of the loop and tape as before. This will enable you to create two sets of stamens from one loop.

5 Cut through the thread using fine scissors. Trim each set if needed to make them shorter.

TINY LOOP

For some flowers, it is useful to create a tiny loop in the bend of the wire prior to threading through the thread loop.

1 Create a tiny loop in the bend of the wire prior to threading through the thread loop.

2 Tape over the thread down onto the wire and cut the thread as before.

3 Open up the thread to reveal the tiny loop at the heart of the stamens.

4 The loop can be used to secure and hold a gum paste ovary.

STAMEN EFFECTS

Cotton thread stamens can be customized further with these effects.

STIFFENED

1 If the stamens need to be stiffened to either add strength or curl them, then dip the prepared thread center into pasteurized or fresh egg white.

2 Blot off any excess with paper towel and then curl using tweezers. Leave to dry.

FUZZY TIPS

You might need to create fuzzy tips to the stamens. If this is the case, simply rub the tips of the thread against an emery board.

AGED

If brown, aged stamen tips are needed, paint the tips. Alternatively, hold the tips over the flame of a tea light to singe them slightly. Be very careful not to hold them in the flame for too long, as the threads will vanish before your very eyes.

Wiring sprays

One of the most satisfying aspects of creating sugar flowers is the process of assembling the flowers and foliage into corsages, posies, sprays, and bouquets. Traditional floristry techniques can be used as a guideline, but you need to take care not to crowd the flowers too tightly, as this might result in the fragile sugar petals being damaged.

Materials

- Nile green florist tape
- 22- and 20-gauge wire

Equipment

- Tape shredder (optional)
- Needle-nose pliers
- Wire cutters or florist's scissors

HOW TO WIRE A SPRAY

The principles behind the wiring of the spray shown here can be used as the basis for creating your own sprays.

1 It is sometimes best to start with the focal flower that you intend to use—in this case, a rose—and work around it. This should be the largest and most attractive flower and it needs to stand higher than any of the other flowers in the bouquet. If the flower needs additional support, simply tape an extra 22- or 20-gauge wire onto its stem using half-width nile green florist tape.

2 Start to add trails of foliage with half-width florist tape. It is best to visualize the bouquet divided into thirds. You will need to use one long length of foliage measuring two-thirds of the length of the total bouquet. Bend the stem at a 90-degree angle using needle-nose pliers and tape this onto the stem of the focal flower, followed by a length of foliage, which will create the remaining third. This will be the start of the "handle" of the bouquet.

3 Next, add the slightly smaller flowers around the focal flower—here, two small roses have been used. Position the first two flowers diagonally opposite each other on either side of the large rose to create a balanced effect.

4 Continue to add more smaller flowers—here, Fantasy Frilly Flowers—and extra foliage to bulk out the middle part of the bouquet. Trim away any excess wire bulk using wire cutters or florist's scissors.

5 Add smaller "filler" flowers—here, jasmine and lily of the valley—to fill in the remaining gaps in the bouquet and soften the edges, aiming to keep a balanced display.

6 Trails and loops of decorative paper-covered wire can be added to give a little extra detail and length to the bouquet. Curl the ends of the wire to soften the edges of the display.

7 Tape over the handle of the bouquet with full-width nile green florist tape to create a neat finish. Use needle-nose pliers to rearrange any of the components that need to be relaxed slightly to create a prettier bouquet.

Attaching flowers

There are a number of different ways of attaching sugar flowers to a cake. They can be wired into a posy, spray, or bouquet and inserted into a food-grade plastic posy pick in the cake. They can be arranged in florist's foam or artist's clay, which is placed on the cake. Or they can be arranged into a vase and displayed on top of a cake. Polystyrene dummy cakes can be used in conjunction with real cakes to hold larger amounts of flowers. Wired flowers should never be inserted directly into a cake.

USING A POSY PICK

You can buy posy picks from most good cake-decorating shops. They are made from food-grade plastic and are available in a few different sizes. Sterilize the posy pick in just-boiled water and wipe with clear alcohol before use.

1 Decide where the spray/bouquet is to be positioned and carefully insert the pick into the cake. It is best to leave the top of the pick raised from the cake's surface, so that it may be removed easily before the cake is cut into slices.

2 Insert the handle of the wired spray/bouquet into the posy pick. For very large bouquets the handle often becomes quite bulky, so you might find it best to use a tapered crystal-effect cake pillar (you will need to cut the length of the handle a little).

3 Once the spray/bouquet is positioned in the posy pick, you will need to readjust the flowers and foliage slightly to create a flowing design for the shape of the cake. Use needle-nose pliers to help you position the items without damaging them.

Materials

- Food-grade plastic posy pick
- Clear alcohol
- Florist's foam or artist's clay
- Piece of food-grade plastic, vase, candle holder, or cake board
- Extra wire

Equipment

- Needle-nose pliers

USING FLORIST'S FOAM OR ARTIST'S CLAY

Arranging flowers into florist's foam or artist's clay is often easier than trying to wire them into a bridal spray. If you make a mistake, it is easy to pull out the flowers and rearrange them. Florist's foam and artist's clay are great mediums for arranging and holding the flowers in place. However, they are not edible and so you will need to secure them onto a piece of food-grade plastic, or into a vase, candle holder, or cake board to separate them from the surface of the cake.

1 To give extra support to the heavier stems, use needle-nose pliers to bend a hook in the end of the wire, then insert firmly into the florist's foam or artist's clay.

2 Use trailing stems of foliage to add length and height to the arrangement. You might find that needle-nose pliers help you to push the stems into hard-to-reach areas of the arrangement.

3 Continue to add smaller flowers and foliage to fill in the gaps around the display.

Sugar flower directory

The directory begins with a beautiful flower selector showing all the flowers in miniature for easy comparison and selection. Once you have chosen the flower you would like to make, turn to the page number indicated, where detailed instructions explain clearly how to make each flower.

Flower selector

Browse the selector, choose the flower you would like to make, then turn to the page indicated for full making instructions.

GARDENIA
Page 112

ROSE
Page 162

PEONY
Page 66

HIBISCUS
Page 128

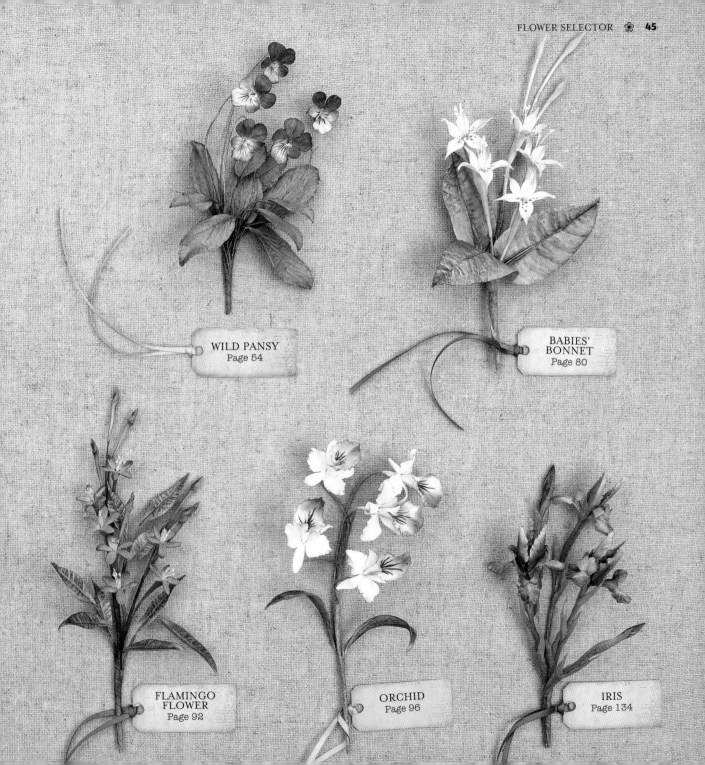

WILD PANSY
Page 54

BABIES'
BONNET
Page 80

FLAMINGO
FLOWER
Page 92

ORCHID
Page 96

IRIS
Page 134

SWEET PEA
Page 74

THISTLE
Page 70

OPIUM POPPY
Page 88

CHINESE
LANTERNS
Page 104

BLUEGRASS
BLOSSOM
Page 84

CHINESE
JASMINE
Page 58

ANEMONE
Page 100

LILY OF THE
VALLEY
Page 50

EASTER LILY
Page 138

PASSION
FLOWER
Page 156

BLUEBELLS
Page 62

GINGER LILY
Page 122

NASTURTIUM
Page 150

CLOWN
ORCHID
Page 108

LISIANTHUS
Page 144

PELARGONIUM
Page 118

Lily of the Valley

This quick lily of the valley (*Convallaria majalis*) is based on Fabergé's pearl lily of the valley, with flakes of mother of pearl for the petals that he used to decorate ornate eggs. Although the flowers are commonly white, there are some varieties that are creamy in color—and pink forms, too. In nature, the flowers have six petals, so you could use a six-petal blossom cutter to make the flowers, but as this is a quick version, a five-petal blossom cutter creates an equally effective representation.

SKILL LEVEL ✿

Materials

- 33- and 24-gauge white wires
- White and mid-green gum paste
- Edible gum glue
- Nile green florist tape
- Vine green, white, foliage green, dark green, and eggplant petal dusts
- Quarter-confectionery glaze (see page 32) or edible glaze spray

Equipment

- Large sharp florist's scissors or wire cutters
- Needle-nose pliers
- Nonstick board
- Nonstick rolling pin
- Tiny five- or six-petal plunger blossom cutter
- Nonstick modeling tool
- Dusting brushes
- X-acto knife or plain-edge cutting wheel
- Double-sided tulip leaf veiner or dried corn husk
- Foam pad
- Large ball tool

BUDS

1 The number of buds varies on each stem—you could make stems consisting of only buds or a combination of buds and flowers. Cut several short lengths of wire using large, sharp florist's scissors or wire cutters. Bend a hook in the end of each wire, using needle-nose pliers.

2 Next, roll a tiny ball of well-kneaded white gum paste and insert a hooked wire into it. Reshape if needed.

3 Repeat to make many buds in graduating sizes. If time allows, leave them to dry before assembly.

Use a five- or six-petal plunger blossom cutter (4).

FLOWERS

4 Cut several short lengths of 33-gauge white wire and hook the end of each as described in step 1. Roll out a small amount of well-kneaded white gum paste very thinly and cut out a blossom shape using a five- or six-petal plunger blossom cutter.

Press the blossom shape into the ball with a nonstick modeling tool (5).

5 Next, quickly roll a small ball of white gum paste to form the main body of the flower. Use the pointed end of a nonstick modeling tool to pick up the blossom shape and quickly press it into the ball to bond the two together. If the gum paste is soft enough, there will be no need to use edible gum glue to stick the two together.

6 Moisten a hooked 33-gauge white wire with edible gum glue and thread it through the center of the flower, embedding the hook into the sides of it. Repeat the process to make between three and seven flowers for each stem. Leave to dry.

1 2 3 4 5 6

Make a hook.

Make three to seven flowers for each stem.

Needle-nose pliers enable you to position the tiny buds and flowers neatly on the stem (7).

ASSEMBLY

7 Tape the buds and flowers onto a 24-gauge white wire using quarter-width nile green florist tape. Start with a tiny bud, leaving a little of its original wire on show, and gradually increase the bud size as you add 10 buds alternating down the stem. Next, add the flowers, again leaving a short amount of the original wire on show.

8 Use needle-nose pliers to bend each flower and bud stem. Use the pliers with a nipping action to create a softer bend in the wire. Once all the flowers and buds have been curved down, use the pliers to pinch and curve the main flower stem.

9 Dust the main stem and the buds with vine green petal dust mixed with white petal dust. The smaller buds should be a stronger green.

LEAVES/FOLIAGE

10 Roll out some well-kneaded mid-green gum paste, leaving a long thick ridge for the wire (see page 22). Cut out the leaf freehand using an X-acto knife or plain-edge cutting wheel (or use the template on page 169).

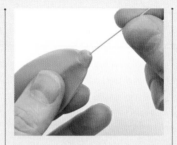

Insert a 24-gauge wire into the ridge of the leaf (11).

11 Insert a 24-gauge white wire moistened with edible gum glue into the thick ridge to support half to two-thirds the length of the leaf.

Here, 33-gauge wires have been used to texture the leaf (12).

12 Next, texture the surface using either a double-sided tulip leaf veiner, a piece of dried corn husk, or a packet of 33-gauge wires curved and pressed into the surface following the curved edges of the leaf.

13 Place the leaf on a firm foam pad and gently soften the edges using a large ball tool. Finally, pick up the leaf and pinch it gently from the base through to the tip to accentuate a central vein. The leaf curls and overlaps slightly at the base, too. Leave the leaf to dry a little before coloring.

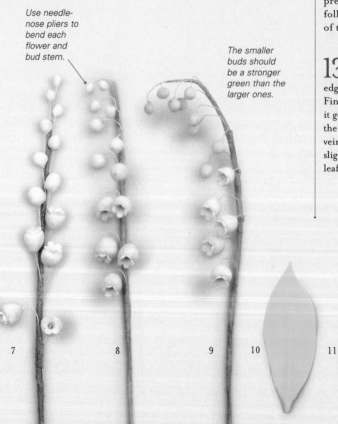

Use needle-nose pliers to bend each flower and bud stem.

The smaller buds should be a stronger green than the larger ones.

7   8   9   10   11

Petal dust locater

Buds
Vine green and
white mix

Leaves
Eggplant
(edges)

Leaves
Layers of vine
green, foliage green,
and dark green

Main stem
Vine green and
white mix

The leaf curls and overlaps slightly at the base (13).

14 The leaf color can vary from quite a bright, fresh green to darker form and there are also variegated varieties. Dust the leaf as desired in layers of vine green, foliage green, and dark green. Add a tinge of eggplant petal dust to the edge of the leaf to define the shape. Dip into a quarter-confectionery glaze, shake off the excess, and leave to dry. Alternatively, spray very lightly with edible glaze spray.

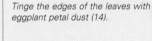

Tinge the edges of the leaves with eggplant petal dust (14).

ASSEMBLY

15 In nature, the bases of the leaves wrap around the stems. However, in sugar this can make it difficult to bend the stems attractively, so it is best to group several stems of flowers and tape the foliage at the base.

13   14

Wild Pansy

Traditionally, the wild pansy (*Viola tricolor*) is a symbol for remembrance and also for love, with folk names like "heartsease," "love-in-idleness," and also "kiss-me-quick"! The wild forms are purple, yellow, and white and any combination of these; however, there are many more colors in the hybridized forms. These flowers can be made without wires to decorate the sides of cakes and cupcakes, but also look great wired in sprays and bouquets, with roses and other wild or cottage garden-style flowers.

SKILL LEVEL ❀ ❀

Materials

- 28- and 26-gauge white wires
- Nile green florist tape
- White and pale green gum paste
- Edible gum glue
- Foliage green, daffodil, sunflower yellow, deep purple, African violet, and dark green petal dusts
- Clear alcohol (optional)
- Black liquid or paste food color or black food color pen
- Quarter-confectionery glaze (see page 32) or edible glaze spray

Equipment

- Needle-nose pliers
- Smooth pointed ceramic tool or dowel
- Fine sharp scissors
- Toothpick (with a sanded blunt end), short wooden skewer, or smooth ceramic tool
- Small nonstick pointed modeling tool or ceramic tool (optional)
- Tiny rose calyx cutter (optional)
- Dresden veining tool
- Nonstick rolling pin
- Grooved board (optional)
- Nonstick board
- Dusting brushes
- Very fine paintbrush
- Small cattleya orchid cutter or template on page 171
- X-acto knife or plain-edge cutting wheel
- Double-sided pansy leaf veiner

Bend a hook in the end of the wire using pliers (1).

Thin out and broaden the shape of each petal (7).

FLOWER

1 Tape over a 28- or 26-gauge white wire with quarter-width nile green florist tape (the gauge will depend on the size of flower you are making. Use needle-nose pliers to bend a hook in the end of the wire.

2 Take a ball of well-kneaded white gum paste and form it into a teardrop shape.

3 Use the pointed end of the smooth ceramic tool or dowel to open up the broad end of the teardrop, thinning the sides of the gum paste against the tool slightly.

4 Next, use fine sharp scissors to cut one large petal and two small petals—one on either side of the large petal—and cut the remainder in half to form two medium-size petals.

5 Open up the petals and then use your finger and thumb to pinch each petal into a point at the tip. Next, flatten each petal between your finger and thumb.

6 Use fine sharp scissors to cut a tiny "V" shape from the central edge of the large petal.

7 Rest the flower on your index finger and use a toothpick, short wooden skewer, or smooth ceramic tool to roll, thin out, and broaden the shape of each petal, increasing the angle of pressure toward the edges.

8 Next, use the pointed end of the ceramic tool to open up the throat of the flower. Use your fingers and thumb to reposition the petals so that the two medium-size petals overlap slightly. Pull and position the two smaller petals forward slightly. Pinch the center of the large heart-shaped petal.

9 Moisten the hooked wire with edible gum glue and thread it through the center of the flower—pierce through behind the two medium-size petals. The hook should be embedded deeply in the center of the flower. Use needle-nose pliers to hold the wire behind the flower and quickly curve the other end of the wire down to create the characteristic bend in the stem. Leave to dry a little before coloring.

2   3   4   Medium x 2   5   6   8   Open up the throat.   9   Insert hooked wire here and bend as shown.

Small x 2   Large   Cut "V" here.

Use a rose calyx cutter to make the calyx (9).

Position the calyx on the back of the flower (11).

Add detail with a very fine paintbrush (13).

Attach florist tape to the stem to represent bracts (14).

CALYX

9 Making a calyx is optional and depends on the detail you have time for. Take a small ball of well-kneaded pale green gum paste and form it into a cone shape. Pinch out the broad end of the cone to create a hat shape (see Babies' bonnet on page 80). Thin out the brim of the "hat" using a small nonstick pointed modeling tool or ceramic tool. Cut out the shape using a tiny rose calyx cutter. Carefully remove the shape from the cutter.

10 Elongate and broaden each sepal slightly. Use the broad end of the dresden veining tool to hollow out the length on the back of each sepal. Pinch the tips of each sepal between your finger and thumb. Open up the center of the calyx using the pointed end of the ceramic tool/nonstick pointed modeling tool.

11 Moisten the inside of the calyx slightly with edible gum glue and position it on the back of the flower. Use fine scissors to cut five tiny sepals into the node of the hat shape. Allow to firm up and dust with foliage green petal dust.

COLORING

12 The coloring will depend on the variety you are copying. Here, the large heart-shape petal is tinged from the center of the flower with a mixture of daffodil and sunflower yellow petal dusts. The outer petals can be dusted with deep purple and African violet, increasing the color on the two medium-size petals. For a very strong coloring, you might find it best to dilute the color with clear alcohol to apply a strong base coat of color. Leave this to dry and then overdust using the same dry color to disguise any streaks.

13 Use a very fine paintbrush and black liquid or paste food color (diluted with clear alcohol or water) to add a series of fine lines on the heart-shaped and two smaller petals.

BRACTS

14 Two bracts may be added to the flower stems. Take a length of quarter-width nile green florist tape and twist it around the stem of the flower. Pinch the tape firmly against the wire to secure it in place—the glue in the tape will be released as you stretch it. Next, use sharp fine scissors to cut away the excess length and trim the bracts into a point. Pinch them to give a little more of a natural shape.

LEAVES

15 Roll out some mid-green gum paste, leaving a thick ridge for the wire—a grooved board may also be used. Cut out a leaf shape using either a small, squashed cattleya orchid cutter or the template on page 171 and an X-acto knife or plain-edge cutting wheel. Insert a 28- or 26-gauge

9

11

12

13

15

16

Insert wire to support half the length of the leaf (15).

Texture the edges of the leaves with the dresden veining tool (16).

white wire moistened with edible gum glue into the ridge to support about half the length of the leaf.

16 Place the leaf against the nonstick board and work the edges at intervals using the broad end of the dresden veining tool, pulling the gum paste against the board.

Line up the tip of the leaf and the wire with the central vein on the veiner (17).

17 Soften the edges and then vein using the double-sided pansy leaf veiner. Remove the leaf from the veiner and pinch it from the base to the tip to accentuate the central vein.

18 Dust the leaf with foliage green petal dust and overdust with dark green fading toward the edges. Dip into a quarter-confectionery glaze or spray lightly with edible glaze spray.

ASSEMBLY

19 Create a natural grouping by adding the foliage at the base or use the flowers individually in sprays with other types of flower.

17

18

Petal dust locater

Outer petals:
Deep purple and
African violet mix

Heart-shaped petal
Daffodil and sunflower
yellow mix (center)

Black (detail)

Leaves
Layers of foliage green
and dark green

Chinese Jasmine

Jasminium polyanthum is a delicate flower to make in sugar that is useful for its pretty flowers and buds, as well as for the plant's foliage in bouquets, sprays, and arrangements, adding an instant touch of elegance. The flowers can be used as filler flowers or as a main feature on celebration cakes and, if made unwired, on couture cupcakes, too!

SKILL LEVEL ❀ ❀

Materials

- 33-, 30-, 28-, and 24-gauge white wires
- White and mid-green gum paste
- Fine stamens (optional)
- Nile green florist tape
- Foliage green, dark green, pale pink, dark pink, and plum petal dusts
- Quarter-confectionery glaze (see page 32) or edible glaze spray

Equipment

- Sharp florist's scissors or wire cutters
- Small sharp scissors
- Nonstick board
- Fine nonstick pointed modeling tool or dowel
- Small five-petal stephanotis cutter
- Foam pad
- Small ball tool
- Dusting brushes
- Rubber leaf or petal veiner

To create a larger bud, pinch a few petals and then twist (3).

You can create five sepals with small sharp scissors, if desired (4).

Cut the flowers with a stephanotis cutter (7).

BUDS

1 You will need to make far more buds than flowers to create a delicate display. Cut several lengths of 33-gauge white wire into quarter lengths using sharp florist's scissors or wire cutters. Take a tiny ball of well-kneaded white gum paste and form it into a cone shape. Insert a 33-gauge white wire into the broad end.

2 Hold the base of the bud between your finger and thumb and firmly work the gum paste down the wire to form a fine elongated neck. Keep the tip of the bud pointed. Trim and remove any excess gum paste from the base of the bud.

3 To create larger slightly unfurling buds, simply pinch a few petals from the tip of the bud, using your finger and thumb. Next, twist the petals back on themselves to create a spiraled effect.

CALYX

4 This step is optional depending on time and the effect you are trying to create. Use a pair of small sharp scissors to snip five tiny sepals at the base of the bud to complete the suggestion of a calyx.

FLOWER

5 Form a small ball of well-kneaded white gum paste into a long teardrop shape. Use your fingers and thumbs to pinch out the broad end of the teardrop to form a wizard's hat shape.

6 Place the shape against the nonstick board and use a fine nonstick pointed modeling tool or dowel to roll out the brim of the hat.

7 Place the small five-petal stephanotis cutter over the thick part of the hat and cut out the flower. The gum paste will probably stick in the cutter—this is good, as it will enable you to pick up both the cutter and flower and use your thumb to rub the gum paste against the cutter to create cleaner edges to the petals. Use the modeling tool to push the flower out of the cutter.

1   2   3   5   6

Twist to create a spiral.

Open the center with the pointed modeling tool (9).

Add a single stamen to the center, if desired (10).

COLORING

12 Dust the quick-snipped calyces on each flower and bud with foliage green petal dust. The buds and flowers can be pure white or tinged a pale or quite dark pink or plum, depending on the effect you are aiming for. Tinge only the upper surface of each bud and flower necks.

LEAVES

13 Cut several short lengths of 30- and 33-gauge white wire (the gauge will depend on the size of the leaf you are making). The leaves can be cut out freehand, with fine, narrow-pointed leaf cutters, or, as here, hand modeled. To hand model, form a fine teardrop-shaped piece of mid-green gum paste and insert a fine wire into the broad end to support half the length. Work the gum paste between your finger and thumb to create a fine, elongated leaf.

14 Place the wired shape against the nonstick board and use the flat side of any rubber leaf/ petal veiner to flatten the shape to make it thinner. It will take practice to create an even and consistent leaf shape. Scissors may be used to neaten and reshape the leaf if needed.

Flatten the leaf shape with the flat side of any veiner (14).

Pinch from the base to the tip (15).

8 Next, place the flower on the palm of your hand or on a firm foam pad, petal side down. Use a small ball tool to thin out and soften the edges of each petal, working half on the paste and half on the foam pad.

9 Use the pointed end of the pointed modeling tool to open up the center of the flower. Next, moisten the end of a 28-gauge white wire and pull it through the center of the flower until it is just hidden. Use your finger and thumb to work/rub the fine back of the flower to create an even finer neck, removing any excess length from the base.

10 If you wish, you may add a single fine stamen into the center of the flower; however, the newly opened flowers tend not to show the stamen too much. Use your finger and thumb to move the petals around a little to add some movement and interest to the flower shape. Add a quick-snipped calyx at the base of the flower, as described in Step 4.

11 Tape over the base of the wire of each bud and flower, using quarter-width nile green florist tape. Next, tape the buds into clusters of varying numbers, using quarter-width nile green florist tape. Add a few flowers to some of the bud clusters.

15 Soften the edges using the small ball tool. Pinch the leaf firmly from the base through to the tip to form a central vein and give the leaf some shape. Repeat the process to make the required number of leaves.

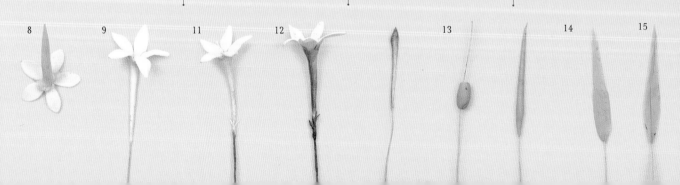

8   9   11   12   13   14   15

Leaves should be taped in pairs down the stem (16).

16
The leaves grow in groups of five, seven, or nine, with the top leaf always being larger than the others. Tape the leaves together using quarter-width nile green florist tape.

17
Dust the leaves with foliage green petal dust. You can add more depth with a darker green. The smaller new-growth foliage is a much brighter green. Dip the leaves into a quarter-confectionery glaze or spray very lightly with edible glaze spray.

ASSEMBLY

18
Tape the leaf sets onto a 24-gauge white wire, using half-width nile green florist tape. The leaf sets should be in pairs down the stem. Add the clusters of buds and flower-and-bud combinations at intervals growing out of the leaf axils. Add more 24-gauge wire as you work down the stem to create length and to support the extra weight.

Petal dust locater

Calyx
Foliage green

Leaves
Layers of foliage green and dark green

Buds and flowers
Pale pink, dark pink, or plum

17

Make one leaf per group larger than the others for a realistic look.

18

Bluebells

A wonderful woodland plant that flowers in the spring, *Hyacinthoides non-scripta* produces mostly blue flowers; however there are also pink and white forms, too. The plant is native to Great Britain and other countries that fringe the Atlantic, but has been introduced as a garden plant in many other parts of the world. The bulbs of the plant were once used to make glue and the starch from the bulbs was used by the Elizabethans to stiffen their elaborate decorative ruffs.

SKILL LEVEL ❁ ❁ ❁

Materials

- 33-, 30-, 28-, 26-, and 24-gauge white wires
- Yellow, deep purple, white, foliage green, and vine green petal dusts
- White gum paste (colored with deep purple petal dust) and mid-green gum paste
- Fine white- or yellow-tipped stamens
- Nontoxic craft glue
- Edible gum glue
- Nile green florist tape
- Quarter-confectionery glaze (see page 32) or edible glaze spray

Equipment

- Antibacterial wipes or clear alcohol and paper tissues
- Florist's scissors or wire cutters
- Plain-edge cutting wheel
- Toothpick or fine-pointed nonstick dowel
- Fine sharp scissors
- Nonstick board
- Fine-pointed modeling tool
- Dusting brushes
- Needle-nose pliers
- Fine paintbrush
- Nonstick rolling pin
- Dresden veining tool
- Dried corn husk or double-sided tulip petal veiner

BUDS

1 First of all you will need to color several lengths of 33- and 30-gauge white wire purple, as well as some 28-gauge wires for the flowers. Use an antibacterial wipe or clear alcohol on a tissue with a little deep purple petal dust to wipe over the wires. Leave the colored wires to dry. Cut them into several shorter lengths using florist's scissors or wire cutters.

2 Color the white gum paste with a little deep purple petal dust. Be careful not to make the paste too dark, as more depth is created later by overdusting with more deep purple petal dust. Roll a small ball of this colored gum paste and insert a purple-colored 33-gauge wire into it. Work the ball into a point at the tip and the base to form a more pointed oval shape.

3 Repeat to make buds in graduating sizes, using colored 33-gauge wire for the smaller buds and 30-gauge wire for the larger buds. If time allows, use a plain-edge cutting wheel to create lines to represent the petals of the flowers.

Open up the center of the flower (7).

STAMENS

4 Take three fine stamens and fold them in half. Use a tiny amount of nontoxic craft glue to bond the stamens together. Leave to set and then cut away the bulk from the bend in the stamens, leaving a short set of stamens.

5 Apply a little glue to the end of a purple-colored 28-gauge wire and attach the stamens to the end, holding firmly to ensure a secure connection. Leave to dry. Repeat to make the required number of stamen centers. If you are using white stamens, dust the tips with yellow petal dust.

Cut in half, then cut each half into three, to form six petals (9).

FLOWERS

6 Take a ball of well-kneaded deep purple-colored gum paste. Form it into a slender cone shape and work the pointed end to form a fine point.

7 Use a toothpick or fine-pointed nonstick dowel to open up the fine pointed end. Work the sides of the opening to create a wider mouth and thin the sides of the flower slightly.

8 Using a pair of fine sharp scissors, make two cuts to create two equal-sized sections.

9 Open up the two sections and then cut each section into three to give the basis for the six petals.

Hold for at least 10 seconds to ensure a secure connection.

2   3   4   5   6   7   8   9

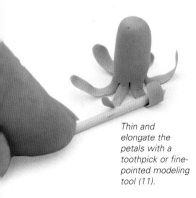

Thin and elongate the petals with a toothpick or fine-pointed modeling tool (11).

Add detail lines using a fine paintbrush (14).

Polish the stems with the side of a pair of scissors (16).

Tinge some of the smaller buds with a mixture of green petal dusts (17).

10 Next, use your finger and thumb to pinch the tip of each petal into a point and then flatten the surface of each petal slightly, too.

11 Place the flower against the nonstick board with the flattened petals face down. Use a blunt toothpick or fine-pointed modeling tool to roll the petals to thin them lengthways and elongate them, too.

12 Pick up the flower and rest it against your index finger. Next, carefully curl each of the petals back on itself to create the characteristic bluebell shape.

13 Moisten the base of the wired stamens with edible gum glue and thread through the center of the flower so that the stamen tips are only just visible. If time allows, use the plain-edge cutting wheel to make lines corresponding to the position and number of petals. Repeat to make at least three flowers per stem. Leave to dry a little.

COLORING AND ASSEMBLY

14 Dust the flowers from the base with a mixture of deep purple and white petal dusts, fading a little toward the edges. Add a little more depth at the base using more deep purple petal dust, if desired. If time allows, extra detail can be added by painting fine lines using a fine paintbrush and a mixture of deep purple petal dust and clear alcohol. Overdust the paintwork to calm it down a little.

15 Use a 26-gauge white wire as the main stem and start by taping the smallest bud onto the end of the wire using quarter-width nile green florist tape. Alternate and graduate the sizes of the buds as you add them, leaving a little of the purple-colored wires on view. Add extra 26- or 24-gauge white wire as you work down the stem to give a fleshier and stronger finish. Gradually add the flowers, too.

16 Use the side of a pair of scissors to rub and polish the stems to create a smoother finish. Use needle-nose pliers to bend each of the buds so that their heads nod downward. Curve the main stem slightly, too.

17 Mix together foliage green and vine green petal dusts, and tinge some of the smaller buds and main stem.

10

11

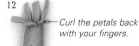

12

Curl the petals back with your fingers.

13

The stamen tips should only just be visible.

14

15

Attach the bracts with edible gum glue (18).

Use a plain-edge cutting wheel to cut out the leaf (20).

BRACTS

18 Tiny bracts may be added at the base of each bud and flower if desired. Roll fine-pointed strands of deep purple gum paste and flatten using your finger or the flat back side of a petal/leaf veiner. Pick up each bract and mark a single line down the middle using a dresden veining tool. Attach each bract at the base of each flower and larger buds using edible gum glue. Overdust with deep purple petal dust. Leave to dry and then hold the stem quickly over a jet of steam from a kettle or a clothes steamer, taking care not to scald yourself.

LEAVES

19 Roll out some mid-green gum paste, leaving a long, thick ridge for the wire. Cut out a long, slender, strap-like leaf shape, using the large end of the plain-edge cutting wheel. Insert a 26- or 24-gauge white wire into the ridge to support at least half the length of the leaf.

20 Texture the leaf using a dried corn husk or double-sided tulip petal veiner. Pinch from the base through to the tip to give a central vein and curve the leaf.

21 Dust in layers of vine green and foliage green petal dusts. Add a gentle tinge of deep purple to the tip and edges of the leaf. Dip into a quarter-confectionery glaze or spray with edible glaze spray.

ASSEMBLY

22 Group together general stems of bluebells and tape together, using half-width nile green florist tape. Add leaves of varying sizes to the base.

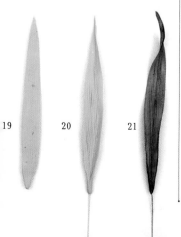

19   20   21

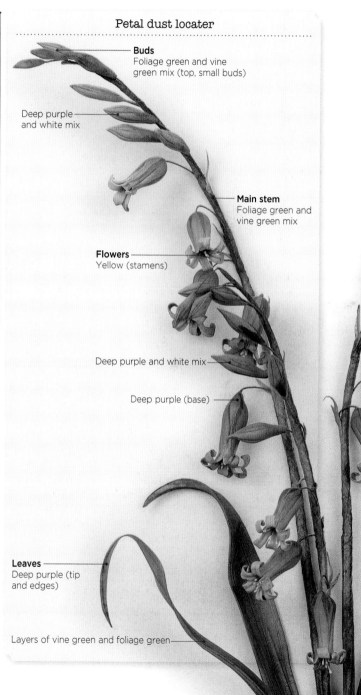

Petal dust locater

Buds
Foliage green and vine green mix (top, small buds)

Deep purple and white mix

Main stem
Foliage green and vine green mix

Flowers
Yellow (stamens)

Deep purple and white mix

Deep purple (base)

Leaves
Deep purple (tip and edges)

Layers of vine green and foliage green

Peony

There are many varieties of peony—the one described here is based on a tree peony. The color range includes soft shades of white, yellow, pink, red, coral, and dark burgundy. Peonies have become a great favorite with sugar-flower artists for use on wedding cakes. The flower's subtle, pastel shades are a perfect match for wedding dress colors.

SKILL LEVEL ❁ ❁ ❁

Materials

- Pale coral, pale green, and mid-green gum paste
- 26- and 24-gauge white wires
- Coral, white, vine green, eggplant, sunflower yellow, and foliage green petal dusts
- Nile green florist tape
- Bunch of white or cream seed-head stamens
- Nontoxic craft glue or edible gum glue
- Edible glaze spray or half-confectionery glaze (see page 32)

Equipment

- Nonstick board
- Nonstick rolling pin
- Large rose petal cutters or templates
- Ceramic silk veining tool or short wooden skewer
- Paper towel
- Dusting brushes
- Needle-nose pliers
- Sharp scissors
- Peony leaf cutter or template on page 173 and X-acto knife
- Large metal ball tool
- Peony leaf veiner

Form a ball of paste into a teardrop shape (1).

PETALS

1 Knead the coral-colored gum paste to make it pliable. Then form a ball of paste into a teardrop shape.

2 Flatten this teardrop shape against the nonstick board.

3 Use a small rolling pin to thin out the paste. Leave a thick ridge down the center to hold a wire (see page 22).

Increase the pressure with the ceramic silk veining tool to frill the edges (5).

4 Cut out the petal shape using the largest rose petal cutter. Insert a hooked, moistened 26-gauge wire into the base of the thick ridge. Carefully push the wire in to support approximately half the length of the petal.

5 Place the petal ridge side up against the board and then texture the surface of the petal in a fan formation, using the ceramic silk veining tool or wooden skewer. It is best to use short rolling actions and then move the tool over the petal and repeat again until the whole surface has a delicate vein. Turn the petal over and repeat on the other side.

6 Next, use the tool with increased pressure on the very edges of the upper curve to create a frilled effect.

7 Place the petal in a paper towel ring former to create a gentle cupped shape. Leave to firm up a little before dusting. Repeat to make a total of 10 large petals and then follow the same process to make five smaller petals, using the slightly smaller rose petal cutter.

8 Mix together coral and a little white petal dust and color each petal from the base, fading out toward the edges on both sides.

1

2   4   5   7   8

Extra coral can be added at the very base to give more depth to the flower if desired.

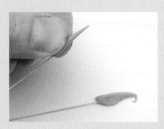

Pinch one side of the carrot shape to create a ridge (11).

Leave the ends of the stamens unglued to allow movement (15).

CARPELS AND STAMENS

9 Cut five short lengths of 26-gauge wire. Use needle-nose pliers to bend a hook in the end of each wire.

10 Roll a small ball of pale green gum paste and insert the hook into it.

11 Use your finger and thumb to work the ball of paste into a slender carrot shape and then pinch a ridge down one side of the shape.

12 Curl the tip of the shape over onto the ridged edge. Repeat to make five carpels.

13 Use quarter-width nile green florist tape to join the five sections together, positioning the ridge on the outer edge. This should be done while the carpels are still malleable, so that you can create a nice, tight shape.

14 Use a flat dusting brush to color the carpels with vine green petal dust. Tinge the tips with a mixture of coral and eggplant petal dust.

15 Take a bunch of white or cream stamens and divide into several smaller groups. Use the nontoxic craft glue or edible gum glue to bond each group together at the center, working the glue toward the tips on either end, remembering to leave a short length on either end unglued to create a realistic stamen effect. Allow the glue to set a little and then use sharp scissors to cut each group in half. Next, trim the shorter groups so that they are a little shorter than the length of the carpels.

16 Using a little more nontoxic or edible gum glue attach the groups of stamens around and onto the base of the carpel center. Usually counting to 10 each time helps to give a good bond between the two pieces. Repeat with the remaining groups to create a circle of stamens around the carpel center. Leave to dry.

17 Dust the tips of the stamens with sunflower yellow petal dust and the filaments (the length) with coral petal dust. The color of the filaments usually corresponds with the color of the flower petals.

ASSEMBLY

18 Use half-width nile green florist tape to assemble the flower. Bend the wire at the base of the petals a little, using needle-nose pliers to help make them fit against the stamens. Start by adding the small petals around the stamens and then add the larger petals filling any gaps in the previous layer of petals.

LEAVES

19 The leaves are usually in sets of three—one large frilled leaf with two smaller hand-like leaves. Roll some mid-green gum paste into a ball. Continue rolling into an elongated sausage shape, then press flat, leaving a thick ridge for the wire.

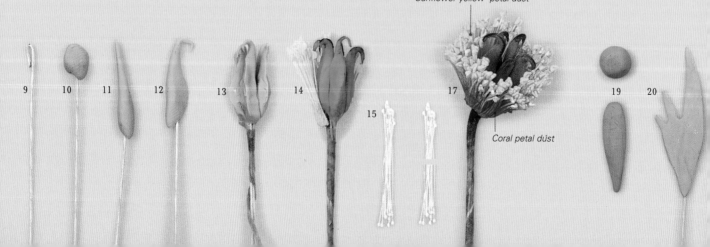

Sunflower yellow petal dust

Coral petal dust

9 10 11 12 13 14 15 17 19 20

20 Cut out the leaf shape using a cutter or the template on page 173 and a X-acto knife. Insert a wire into the thick ridge of the leaf to support about half the length of the leaves. The exact gauge will depend on the size of the leaf. The larger leaves need a 24-gauge wire, medium and small leaves will need a 26-gauge wire to support them.

21 Place the leaf on your palm or on a foam pad and soften the "cut" edge using the metal ball tool. Roll the tool half on the paste and half on the pad. Next, vein the leaf using the peony leaf veiner. Remove from the veiner and pinch the leaf gently from the base through to the tip to create a stronger central vein and some movement. Repeat to make three leaves.

22 Dust the leaves, layering on the color. Use foliage green for the base fading out toward the edges. Over dust with vine green petal dust and then finally tinge the edges of the leaves using eggplant petal dust.

23 Spray lightly with edible glaze spray or dip into a half-confectionery glaze (see page 32), shake, and allow to dry. Tape the three leaves together using half-width nile green florist tape—the large tri-lobed leaf in the center with the two smaller leaves on either side.

ASSEMBLY

24 Tape the sets of leaves onto the stem of the flower using half-width nile green florist tape. Start with a small set of leaves directly behind the flower and gradually increase the size of the foliage as you work down the stem.

Petal dust locater

Stamens
Sunflower yellow (tips)

Coral (filaments)

Carpels
Vine green

Coral and eggplant mix (tips)

Petals
Coral and white mix

Leaves
Layers of foliage green and vine green

Eggplant (edges)

21

Pinch here.

23

Thistle

The method described here creates a very quick and effective version of the thistle. The fine petals of the flower can be made with sugar, but they tend to be very fragile and time-consuming to make. In this version, fine cotton thread is used to create the plume—an iconic symbol for all things Scottish!

SKILL LEVEL ✿

Materials

- Fine cotton lacemaker's thread (gauge 120)
- 26-gauge white wires
- Nile green florist tape
- African violet or violet, foliage green, eggplant, and white bridal satin petal dusts
- Plastic bag
- Hairspray (optional)
- Pale to mid-green gum paste
- Edible gum glue
- Quarter-confectionery glaze (see page 32) or edible glaze spray

Equipment

- Fine sharp scissors
- Emery board
- Smooth ceramic tool or nonstick pointed modeling tool
- Nonstick rolling pin
- Thistle leaf cutter or template on page 169
- X-acto knife
- Foam pad
- Ball tool or bone end tool
- Dresden veining tool or plain-edge cutting wheel
- Dusting brushes

PETAL PLUME

1 Take a reel of fine cotton lacemaker's thread and wrap it around two parted fingers between 60 and 100 times (depending on how large you intend your thistle to be).

2 Remove the large loop from your fingers and then twist it to form a figure-eight shape.

3 Next, fold the figure-eight to form a smaller loop. Take a 26-gauge white wire and bend it through the loop to hold it in place—do not twist the wire.

4 Tape over the base of the thread and down onto the wire using quarter-width nile green florist tape. If the loop of thread is large enough, you can create two sets by threading, bending, and taping another wire opposite the original wire.

5 Use sharp scissors to cut the thread loop in half. Trim the threads to the desired length—again, this will depend on the effect you want to achieve. The thistles pictured here are based on a smaller variety.

6 Use an emery board to "fluff" up the tips of the thread, which will create a softer effect and also bulk up the appearance.

Rub the tips of the thread against an emery board to create a fluffy look (6).

Color the plume with African violet petal dust (7).

7 Dip the fluffed-up plumes into a pot of African violet or violet petal dust to color thoroughly. Place the piece inside a plastic bag to blow off the excess color. You may seal the color on the threads using hairspray, but this can only be done if the flowers are not being held too close to the cake.

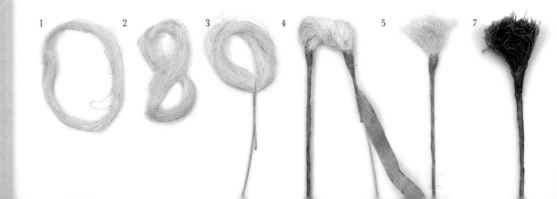

1   2   3   4   5   7

CALYX

8 Take a ball of well-kneaded pale to mid-green gum paste and form it into a cone shape.

9 Use the pointed end of the smooth ceramic tool or nonstick pointed modeling tool to open up the fine end of the cone shape.

10 Thread the wire thread plume through the center of the hollowed-out cone.

11 Squeeze the opening of the cone against the thread plume.

12 Next, squeeze the main body of the cone to create the desired bulk and depth. Work the excess gum paste down the wire between your finger and thumb and remove any excess.

Cut the spines with sharp curved scissors (13).

13 Turn the thistle upside down and, using a fine pair of sharp curved scissors, cut and create the characteristic thistle spines by placing the scissors close to the surface and making as many fine cuts as you can. Carefully flick and curve some of the cut sections back slightly.

LEAVES

14 Roll out some well-kneaded pale to mid-green flower paste, leaving a thick ridge for the wire (see page 22). Cut the leaf using a thistle leaf cutter or the template on page 169 and an X-acto knife. Insert a length of 26-gauge white wire moistened with edible gum glue into the thick ridge to support half to two-thirds the length of the leaf.

Mark a central vein on each leaf (16).

15 Place the leaf on a firm foam pad or the palm of your hand and soften and thin the edges using a ball tool or bone end tool.

16 Use a dresden veining tool or plain-edge cutting wheel to mark a central vein on each section. Pinch the leaf from the base through the tip and curve the length of the leaf slightly. Repeat to make several leaves for each thistle.

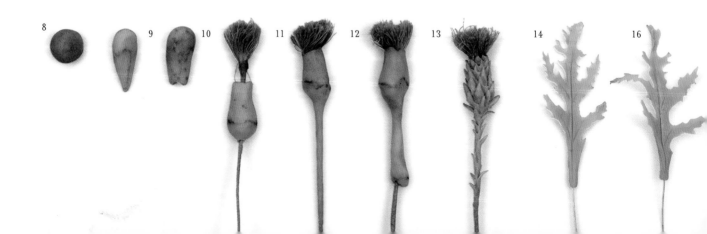

Overdust the leaves with white bridal satin petal dust (17).

COLORING

17 Dust the spiky calyx and the leaves with foliage green petal dust. Add tinges of eggplant to the spikes if desired. Overdust with white bridal satin petal dust. Glaze the leaves and calyx lightly with quarter-confectionery glaze or spray with edible glaze spray.

ASSEMBLY

18 Tape the leaves onto the thistle stems using half-width nile green florist tape. Dust over the stems using foliage green and white bridal satin petal dust.

17   18

Petal dust locater

Plumes — African violet or violet

Calyx — Foliage green

Eggplant (edges)

White bridal satin

Leaves — Foliage green

Eggplant (edges)

White bridal satin —

Sweet pea

Sweet peas (*Lathyrus odoratus*) are often taught as a beginner's flower. Here, the method described has individually wired petals giving more strength to what is generally quite a fragile sugar flower. The color range and combinations are vast, making them a very useful flower for cake design.

SKILL LEVEL ❀ ❀

Materials

- 20-, 22-, 24-, 28-, and 30-gauge white wires
- White and pale green gum paste
- Edible gum glue
- Nile green florist tape
- Daffodil, vine green, white, African violet, plum, eggplant, and foliage green petal dusts
- Quarter-confectionery glaze (see page 32) or edible glaze spray

Equipment

- Needle-nose pliers
- Nonstick rolling pin
- X-acto knife or plain-edge cutting wheel
- Two small rose petal cutters or templates on page 170
- Fine sharp scissors
- Short wooden skewer or ceramic silk veining tool
- Foam pad
- Dresden veining tool
- Nonstick board
- Small nonstick pointed modeling tool or ceramic tool (optional)
- Small rose calyx cutter
- Sweet pea petal cutters— wing petal and standard petal or templates on page 168
- Toothpicks
- Dusting brushes
- Ball tool
- Fine peony leaf veiner (optional)
- Paintbrush

KEEL

1 The center of a sweet pea is known as the keel. Bend a hook in the end of a 24-gauge white wire using needle-nose pliers. Form a ball of well-kneaded white gum paste into a teardrop shape. Moisten the hook with edible gum glue and insert it into the base of the cone. Work the base between your finger and thumb to create a slightly tapered shape.

2 Next, pinch down the length of one side of the cone to create a subtle ridge and flatten the sides slightly too. Use an X-acto knife or plain-edge cutting wheel to indent the straight edge to represent the opening in the keel petal. Curve the straight edge back slightly. You will need to make a keel for each flower and each bud, the smaller buds requiring slightly smaller keels.

BUDS

3 Thinly roll out some well-kneaded white gum paste and cut out two rose petal shapes of the same size (this will depend on the size of bud you are making, as they graduate in size down the stem).

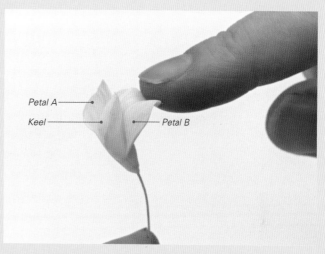

Petal A
Keel
Petal B

Buds are constructed from a keel and two petals (7).

4 Use an X-acto knife, fine sharp scissors, or a plain-edge cutting wheel to make a deep, narrow "V"-shaped cut in one of the petals (petal A).

5 Use a short wooden skewer or ceramic silk veining tool to roll over the two sections of petal A and then increase the pressure on the edge to frill slightly. Next, moisten with edible gum glue at the base and attach over the keel. Pinch the petal into place to secure the keel and the petal together.

6 Vein and frill the second petal (petal B) as in step 5. Place on a firm foam pad or on your palm and use the fine end of the dresden veining tool to mark a central vein.

7 Next, attach petal B to petal A and the keel, pinching them together firmly at the base to secure them in place. Use your finger to curl the petal B back very slightly on the top central edge. Repeat to make buds of varying sizes. Leave to dry a little before coloring.

1 2 3 4 5 6 7

Petal A

Petal B

Pinch at the base to secure the keel, petal A, and petal B together

CALYX

8 Form a small ball of well-kneaded mid-green gum paste into a teardrop shape. Pinch out the broad end to form a "hat" shape. Place the shape flat against the nonstick board and thin out around the "brim" using a small nonstick or ceramic modeling tool.

9 Use a small rose calyx cutter or the template on page 168 and an X-acto knife to cut out the calyx shape and position the thick node at the center of the shape. Usually the gum paste sticks in the cutter, but this can be used to your advantage! Pick up the cutter and rub your thumb against the edges of the cutter shape—this will create a cleaner cut edge. Remove the shape from the cutter and place it back against the nonstick board. Use the nonstick or ceramic modeling tool to roll and elongate each of the five sepals slightly.

Thread the calyx onto the wire with the petals (11).

10 Place the calyx on a firm foam pad flat side down and use the broad end of the dresden veining tool to hollow out the length of each sepal. Use the pointed end of the nonstick or ceramic modeling tool to open up the center of the calyx.

11 Moisten the center with edible gum glue and thread onto the back of the bud. Position two of the sepals on the back of the outer petal. Smooth and thin the back if it needs it and remove any excess length. Pinch and curl the tips of the calyx back slightly.

Use needle-nose pliers to create a graceful bend in the wire (12).

12 Tape over the stem with half-width nile green florist tape. Use needle-nose pliers to bend the stem. Hold the stem directly behind the calyx and then hold the other end of the wire between your finger and thumb, bending it over in a long, swift and confident swoop to create a neat curve in the top of the stem.

FLOWER—WING PETALS

13 You will already have the keel made from earlier, as described in steps 1 and 2. The next stage is to create two wing petals to sit either side of the keel. Roll out some well-kneaded white gum paste, leaving a thick ridge down the center. Cut out a wing petal using either the sweat pea wing petal cutter or the template on page 168 and an X-acto knife.

14 Insert a 30-gauge white wire moistened with edible gum glue into the thick ridge to support about a third of the length. Pinch the base of the petal onto the wire to firmly secure the two together.

    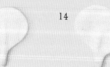 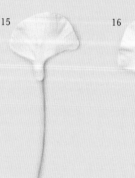

8   9   10   13   14   15   16

Texture with the silk veining tool (15).

15 Place the petal against the nonstick board and texture the surface by gently rolling the silk veining tool in a fan formation over the petal; increase the pressure on the edge of the petal. An extra-fine frilled edge can be achieved using a blunt toothpick or short wooden skewer (see page 13). Repeat the process to make a left and a right wing petal.

16 Leave them to firm up just a little before taping them onto either side of a wired keel using quarter-width nile green florist tape. As the petals are still pliable at this stage, you should be able to manipulate them to create a more realistic effect.

FLOWER—STANDARD PETAL

17 Roll out some more white gum paste, leaving a thick ridge for the wire. Cut out the petal using either the large cutter from the sweet pea set or an X-acto knife and the template on page 168. Moisten a 28-gauge white wire with edible gum glue and insert it into the base of the petal.

18 Vein the petal and frill as for the wing petals, working the silk veining tool in a fan formation.

19 Place the petal on a firm foam pad and use the fine end of the dresden veining tool to mark a central vein down the petal. Turn the petal over and, using the broad end of the dresden veining tool, hollow out two small indents at the base on either side of the central vein: this will create two small bumps on the front of the petal. Leave to firm up a little, drying over a gentle curve.

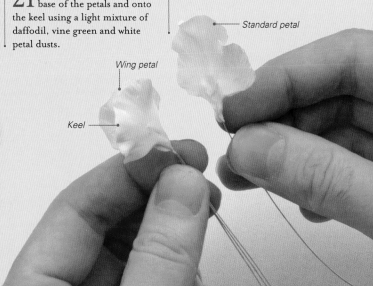

Hollow out two small indents at the base of the standard petal (19).

20 Tape the standard petal tightly to the back of the wired wing petals, using half-width nile green florist tape. Squeeze the base of the petals together to form a neat, tight connection. Curl back the standard petal, remembering that the more mature flowers curve further back than the newer blooms. Leave to dry a little before the final coloring.

COLORING

21 Add a "glow" of color at the base of the petals and onto the keel using a light mixture of daffodil, vine green and white petal dusts.

Work from the edges toward the base in your chosen color (22).

22 Next, add your chosen color, working from the edges toward the base of each petal. Here, the purple flowers were dusted with a mixture of African violet and white petal dusts, and the pink flowers were dusted with plum. The darker variety is a mixture of plum and eggplant.

17

19

20

Standard petal

Wing petal

Keel

Add a calyx, then color with petal dust (23).

LEAVES

25 The leaves grow in pairs on trailing stems along with the plant's tendrils. Roll out some mid-green gum paste, leaving a thick ridge for the wire (see page 22). Cut out the leaf using the leaf template on page 168 and an X-acto knife. Alternatively, they are quite straightforward in shape to cut out freehand with a little practice.

26 Insert a 28-gauge white wire moistened with edible gum glue into the thick ridge to support about half the length of the leaf.

27 Place the leaf on your palm or a firm foam pad and soften the edges using the ball tool. Next, texture the leaf using a fine peony leaf veiner or freehand using the plain-edge cutting wheel.

Use a toothpick to frill the edges of the leaves, if desired (28).

28 The edges of the leaves vary between varieties—some have a fairly flat edge while others are quite frilly. To create the latter, use a toothpick to frill the edges. Pinch the leaf from the base to the tip to accentuate a central vein. Repeat to make leaves in pairs of graduating sizes.

29 Dust the leaves in layers, first using foliage green and then a mixture of vine green and white petal dusts. Leave to dry, then steam the leaves to set the color or dip into a quarter-confectionery glaze or spray lightly with edible glaze spray. The natural leaves are not at all shiny, but sometimes the sugar version looks better with a slight glaze.

23 Add the calyx as for the bud (see Steps 8–12). Dust the calyx with a mixture of foliage green, vine green and a touch of white petal dusts. Curve the stem as described in Step 12.

ASSEMBLY

24 Tape the buds and flowers onto a 20-gauge white wire, using half-width nile green florist tape. There are usually three or four flowers on each stem.

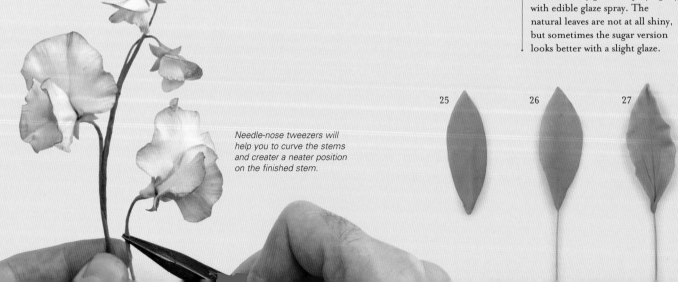

Needle-nose tweezers will help you to curve the stems and creater a neater position on the finished stem.

25   26   27

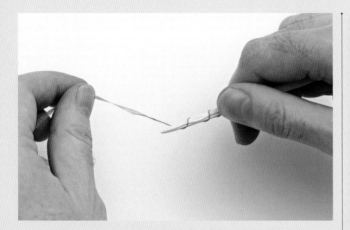

TENDRILS

30 The tendrils grow from the leaf stems and are not attached to the flowers—a common mistake made among flower makers. Use quarter-width nile green florist tape and twist it back on itself to form fine strands. You will need three of these fine strands to form one group. Tape the three tendrils onto the end of a 24-gauge white wire, using half-width florist tape. Add the leaves in pairs, graduating in size down the stems. Tape in extra 22-gauge white wire for longer stems. Curl the tendrils gently around a paintbrush handle.

Twist quarter-width florist tape back on itself and then curl around a paintbrush handle to create the tendrils (30).

ASSEMBLY

31 Sweet peas can be combined with other flowers in sprays and arrangements. However, they are often at their best by themselves in mixed color combinations in tied bunches accompanied by their trailing foliage stems and tendrils, as here.

29   30

Petal dust locater

Flower center
Daffodil, vine green, and white mix

Calyx
Foliage green, vine green, and white mix

Leaves
Layers of foliage green and vine green and white mix

Pink flowers
Plum

Purple flowers
African violet and white mix

Maroon flowers
Plum and eggplant mix

Babies' Bonnet

This method of creating a flower from a "hat" shape can be applied to both fantasy flowers and botanical specimens. The flower pictured is a fantasy form that features nontoxic glitter stamens and tips. The possibilities of color combinations are endless.

SKILL LEVEL ❀

Materials

- White and mid-green gum paste
- 26-gauge white wires
- White seed-head stamens
- Nontoxic craft glue
- Pale green nontoxic craft glitter
- Edible gum glue
- Nile green florist tape
- Coral, white, bluegrass, foliage green, eggplant, and white bridal satin petal dusts
- Clear alcohol
- Half-confectionery glaze (see page 32) or edible glaze spray

Equipment

- Fine sharp scissors
- Nonstick board
- Nonstick pointed modeling tool
- Rose calyx cutter or template on page 169
- Smooth ceramic tool
- Dresden veining tool
- Dusting brushes and fine paintbrush
- Nonstick rolling pin
- Plain-edge cutting wheel
- Foam pad
- Large ball tool
- Large double-sided leaf veiner

Add nontoxic craft glitter to the stamens (3).

BUDS

1 Form a cone of white gum paste. Insert a 26-gauge white wire in the broad end. Thin and elongate the base of the shape down the wire to create a long slender neck.

STAMENS

2 Take three seed-head stamens and trim off their tips from one end using fine sharp scissors. Stagger their position slightly and use a tiny amount of nontoxic craft glue to bond them together. Leave to set for a few minutes and then attach them, using a little more glue on the end of a 26-gauge white wire. Leave to set. Repeat to make as many sets as required. It is best to do this in advance of forming the flowers, so that a good firm connection is created.

Roll out the brim of the hat (5).

3 Apply a tiny amount of nontoxic craft glue to the stamen tips and dip into pale green nontoxic craft glitter.

FLOWER

4 Take a ball of well-kneaded white gum paste and form it into a long teardrop shape. Pinch out the broad end between your fingers and thumbs to create a hat shape.

5 Place the "hat" on the nonstick board and roll out around the brim using the nonstick pointed modeling tool.

Use the pointed end of the smooth ceramic tool to push the flower shape from the cutter (6).

6 Place the rose calyx cutter or the template on page 169 over the central part of the hat and cut out the flower shape. The gum paste usually sticks in the cutter at this stage, which you can use to your advantage as this will allow you to rub your thumb against the paste on the edge of the cutter to create a cleaner cut edge. Use the pointed end of the smooth ceramic tool to push the flower shape out of the cutter.

1   2   4   6

Stagger the position of the seed heads.

Mark a central vein onto each petal (8).

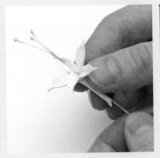

Thread the wired stamens through the center of the flower (9).

Tape over the wire with quarter-width florist tape (10).

Paint a series of very fine dots onto the petals (12).

7 Place the flower with the petals flat on the nonstick board. Use either the nonstick pointed modeling tool or the smooth ceramic tool to slightly elongate and broaden each petal, leaving a slight ridge at the length of each petal.

8 Rest the flower on your index finger and, using the fine end of the dresden veining tool, mark a central vein on each petal. Next, pinch the tips of each petal into a finer point.

9 Moisten the base of the wired stamens very lightly with edible gum glue and then thread the wire through the center of the flower.

10 Work the back of the flower between your finger and thumb to create a long, slender neck. Pinch off any excess length. Tape over the wire, using quarter-width nile green florist tape.

COLORING

11 As this is a fantasy flower, you can allow your creative instinct to guide you. Here, the backs of the flowers and the very edges of the petals have been dusted with a mixture of coral and white petal dusts. Use a fine brush to add a tinge of bluegrass mixed with white at the very center of the flower.

12 Dilute coral petal dust with clear alcohol and paint a series of very fine dots onto the petals.

7

8

10

11

14

Dust the buds with coral and white petal dust (13).

13 Dust the buds with the same coral and white petal dust mixture used for the flower.

ASSEMBLY

14 Use half-width nile green florist tape to assemble the buds together—alternate their position as you work down the stem. Gradually introduce the flowers.

LEAVES

15 Roll out some mid-green gum paste, leaving a thick ridge for the wire. Use the plain-edge cutting wheel to cut out a large ovate-shaped leaf. Insert a 26-gauge white wire into the central ridge to support about half the length of the leaf. Place the leaf on a firm foam pad and soften the edges using a large ball tool.

16 Place into a large double-sided leaf veiner—here, a mandevilla leaf has been used. Press the two sides together to give a good impression. Remove from the veiner and pinch the leaf from the base to the tip to accentuate the central vein. Leave to dry a little before coloring.

17 Dust the leaf in layers of foliage green and a little bluegrass mixed with white bridal satin dust. Add a tinge of coral and eggplant to the edges. Dip into a half-confectionery glaze or spray lightly with edible glaze spray.

18 Use half-width nile green florist tape to add the leaves to the buds and flowers.

Petal dust locater

Buds
Coral and white mix

Flowers
Bluegrass and white mix (center)

Coral (detail)

Coral and white mix (backs and edges)

Leaves
Layers of foliage green and bluegrass and white bridal satin mix

Coral and eggplant mix (edges)

15 16 17

Bluegrass Blossom

These fantasy frilled flowers are very quick and fairly easy to make. This style of flower is often taught as a beginner's flower to illustrate the technique of making flowers without cutters. The flower can be made in any color you wish. Here, the flowers have been made in a fantasy aqua color and assembled with foliage as if they belong to a climbing plant. However, the flowers may also be used without foliage and as filler flowers in sprays.

SKILL LEVEL ❀

Materials

- Stamens
- Nontoxic craft glue
- 28-, 26-, and 22-gauge white wires
- White and pale green gum paste
- Bluegrass, white, eggplant, foliage green, and white bridal satin petal dusts
- Edible gum glue
- Nile green florist tape
- Half-confectionery glaze (see page 32) or edible glaze spray

Equipment

- Wire cutters or sharp florist's scissors
- Needle-nose pliers (optional)
- Nonstick pointed modeling tool, smooth pointed ceramic tool, or sharpened dowel
- Toothpick, short wooden skewer (cut down to size), or ceramic (or plastic) silk veining tool
- Fine sharp scissors
- Dusting brushes
- Tweezers
- Nonstick board
- Double-sided rose leaf veiner
- Foam pad
- Ball tool

Hollow out the broad end of the teardrop shape (3).

FLOWERS

1 Take six stamens grouped together. Fold them in half and bond them together with a little nontoxic craft glue. Leave to set and then trim away the excess bulk and length using fine sharp scissors. Attach one group of stamens to the end of a 26-gauge wire using a little nontoxic craft glue and leave to dy. Repeat to make the required number of stamen centers.

2 Decide if you want to color the gum paste to a base color or leave it white. Here, a little bluegrass petal dust has been kneaded into white gum paste. Take a small ball of this colored gum paste and form it into a teardrop shape, using your finger and thumb.

Use sharp scissors to cut five petals (4).

3 Next, hollow out the broad end of the teardrop using the pointed end of the nonstick pointed modeling tool, smooth pointed ceramic tool or a sharpened dowel.

4 Remove the tool and then cut the required number of petals—here, five even-sized petals have been created.

5 Open up the petals and then pinch each petal into a slightly pointed shape using your finger and thumb.

6 Next, flatten each petal to thin out the shape a little.

Pinch, then flatten each petal (6).

Thin out and texture each petal (7).

7 Rest the flower against your index finger and, using a toothpick, cut-down short wooden skewer, or silk veining tool broaden, texture and thin out each petal to create a much finer frilly effect.

8 Once all the petals have been frilled, remove the flower from your finger and use the pointed end of the smooth ceramic or nonstick modeling tool to open up the center of the flower.

 1   2   3   4   5 6 7

9 Take a wired stamen, moisten it with edible gum glue, and thread it through the center of the flower. Use your finger and thumb to roll and thin out the back of the flower, creating a slender neck shape. Pinch off any excess length that is created in the process. Flick and move the petals around a little into a slightly spiraled effect to create a more pleasing shape and a little movement. Repeat to make the required number of flowers.

BUDS

10 Cut several short lengths of 28-gauge white wire. Take a small ball of well-kneaded bluegrass-colored gum paste and form it into a teardrop shape. Insert a wire into the broad end of the shape.

11 Use your finger and thumb to work the base of the cone shape down the wire to create a tapered neck.

Pinch three petals, then twist together to form a bud (12).

12 Use tweezers or your fingers to pinch out three petals from the upper part of the bud shape. Thin each section between your finger and thumb and then twist the petals back on themselves to create a spiral effect. Repeat to make buds in varying sizes. Use quarter-width nile green florist tape to tape over each flower and bud stem.

COLORING

13 Mix together white and bluegrass petal dusts. Use a flat dusting brush to apply color to the back of the flowers and then catch the edges of the petals and the stamen tips slightly, too. Use the same mixture to tinge the buds with color.

Use a flat dusting brush to dust the back of the flowers (13).

14 Use another brush to tinge the edges of the flower and bud petals, the stamen tips, and the base of each flower and bud with eggplant petal dust.

LEAVES

15 Form a long teardrop of pale green gum paste and insert a 28-gauge white wire into the broad end, so that it supports at least half the length of the shape.

16 Place it against the nonstick board and use the flat side of the double-sided rose leaf veiner to flatten and thin out the shape. This will increase the size of the shape and you might find that you will need to neaten and trim the edges slightly, using sharp scissors.

17 Place the leaf on your palm or on a firm foam pad and thin out the edges using the ball tool. Work the tool half on the gum paste and half on your palm/pad. Next, place it in the double-sided rose leaf veiner, lining up the tip and the base of the leaf with the central vein of the veiner. Press the top half of the veiner on top to give a firm imprint of the leaf texture.

18 Remove the leaf from the veiner and pinch it from the base through to the tip to accentuate the central vein and curve the leaf tip slightly. Repeat to make two smaller leaves to position on either side of the larger central leaf. Repeat to makes leaf groups in varying sizes.

19 Tape each leaf stem/wire using quarter-width nile green florist tape and then tape two smaller leaves on either side of a large leaf.

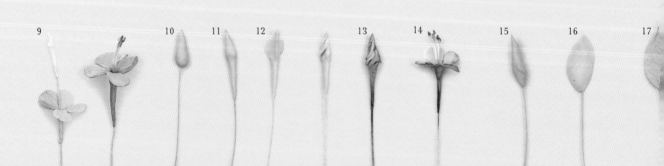

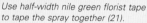

Use half-width nile green florist tape to tape the spray together (21).

Tinge the edges of the leaves with eggplant petal dust (20).

20 Dust the leaves in layers, starting with white bridal satin dust and then a little foliage green petal dust. Tinge the edges with eggplant petal dust. Dip into a half-confectionery glaze or spray with edible glaze spray.

ASSEMBLY

21 Tape the buds and flowers into small clusters, using half-width nile green florist tape. Next, create a trailing stem using a 22-gauge wire as the main stem. Tape a small set of leaves to the end of the wire using half-width nile green florist tape. Continue adding sets of leaves down the stem. Attach clusters of buds and flowers at leaf axils. Increase the size of the foliage a little as you work down the stem.

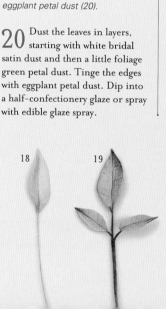

18   19

Petal dust locater

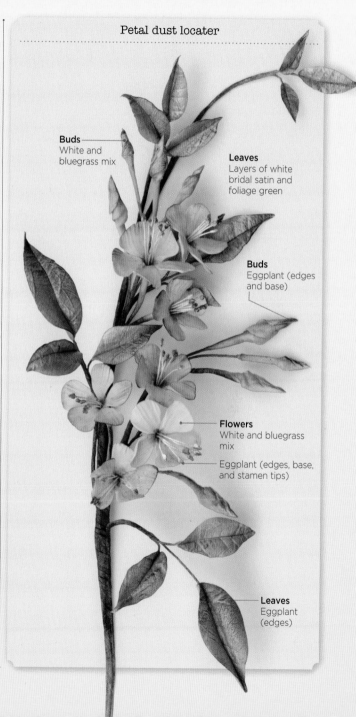

Buds
White and bluegrass mix

Leaves
Layers of white bridal satin and foliage green

Buds
Eggplant (edges and base)

Flowers
White and bluegrass mix

Eggplant (edges, base, and stamen tips)

Leaves
Eggplant (edges)

Opium Poppy

The opium poppy (*Papaver somniferum*) has been grown as a valuable farming plant for centuries. The seeds of the opium poppy (not the narcotic variety!) are used in breads and cakes, particularly in central Europe. The seeds can also be crushed to create an oil suitable for cooking and in the manufacture of paint, varnish, and soap. The large, beautiful flowers are also grown as ornamental garden plants prized for their wonderful seed heads. The flowers vary in size and depth of color, with some varieties being white or red and others having fringed edges. Poppies are wonderful flowers for newcomers to flower-making as they only have four petals (mostly), making them fairly quick and versatile flowers to add to your repertoire.

SKILL LEVEL ❀ ❀

Materials

- White and pale green gum paste
- 28-, 26-, 22-, and 20-gauge white wires
- Edible gum glue
- Plum, African violet, white, eggplant, vine green, daffodil, black, sunflower yellow, foliage green, and forest green petal dusts
- Small white stamens
- Nontoxic craft glue or edible gum glue
- Clear alcohol
- Nile green florist tape
- Quarter-confectionery glaze (see page 32) or edible spray varnish

Equipment

- Nonstick board
- Nonstick rolling pin
- Poppy petal cutters or templates on page 169
- X-acto knife or plain-edge cutting wheel
- Double-sided poppy petal veiner or similar fan-formation veiner (see page 25 to make your own)
- Ceramic silk veining tool
- Toothpick or short wooden skewer
- Large ball tool
- Flat dusting brush
- Needle-nose pliers
- Fine-angled tweezers
- Fine paintbrush
- Scriber or texturing wire brush
- Poppy or coleus leaf cutter or template on page 169
- Dresden veining tool
- Double-sided cyclamen or thistle leaf veiner

Cut the petals from well-kneaded gum paste (1).

Press firmly on the double-sided poppy petal veiner to texture (4).

Add deep eggplant petal dust to the inside of the base of the petal (6).

PETALS

1 Roll out some well-kneaded white gum paste, leaving a thick ridge for the wire (see page 22)—the edges of the gum paste need to be very fine. Cut out a large petal, using the large poppy petal cutter from the poppy set or the template on page 169 and an X-acto knife or plain-edge cutting wheel.

2 Insert a 26-gauge white wire moistened with edible gum glue into the thick ridge to support about a third to half the depth of the petal. Pinch the petal firmly at the base onto the wire.

3 Place the petal back on the nonstick board and thin the edges, using a small, nonstick rolling pin.

4 Place the petal into the double-sided poppy petal veiner and press firmly to texture both sides of the petal. Alternatively, use a homemade fan-effect veiner (see page 25) and vein the petal on the front, then turn it over and vein the back.

5 Frill the edges of the petals using the ceramic silk veining tool. This may be done on the nonstick board or against your index finger. For an even finer edge, frill using a toothpick or short wooden skewer.

6 Use the large ball tool to hollow the center of the petal very gently. Repeat to make another large petal and two smaller petals (these will need 28-gauge white wires).

COLORING

6 It is best to color the petals with petal dust before they have a chance to dry, so that the color sticks well. Mix together plum, African violet, and white petal dusts. Dust the petals from the edges and then from the base at back and front using the petal dust mixture and the flat dusting brush. Next, add a deep eggplant marking on the inside of the petal at the base. The back also shows this dark color, but it will be slightly paler than the inside.

2

3

4

6

Try not to misshape the petal as you work on it.

Pinch the ridges on the ovary with fine-angled tweezers (8).

Use a flat dusting brush to color the ridges of the ovary (10).

Tape two small petals opposite each other, then two large petals in the gaps (14).

OVARY

7 Bend a hook in the end of a 22-gauge white wire using needle-nose pliers. Roll a small piece of well-kneaded pale green gum paste into a ball. Insert the hook into the base of the ball and pinch the gum paste down onto the wire to secure the two together.

8 Using your fingers and thumb, flatten the top of the ovary and pinch a gentle ridge around the circumference. Create the wheel-like spoke formation on the top of the ovary using fine-angled tweezers to pinch eight to 10 ridges radiating from the center.

9 Next, use the pointed end of the ceramic silk veining tool to gently indent in between each "spoke."

10 Mix together vine green, daffodil, and a touch of white petal dusts. Use the flat dusting brush to catch the ridges with color. Leave to dry.

STAMENS

11 Take a bunch of small white stamens, divide them into much smaller groups of five to 10, and line up their tips. Use a little nontoxic craft glue to bond the stamens together at the center, working the glue between your finger and thumb to create a neat line securing the stamens together but leaving a little of either end near the tips unglued. Leave the glue to dry for a few minutes, then cut the stamens in half and trim each half to create shorter groups of stamen.

12 Apply a tiny amount of nontoxic craft glue or edible gum glue to attach the small groups of stamen around the ovary. Pinch each group firmly against the ovary to secure it in place. Once a nice ring of stamens has been created, leave the center to dry. Use fine-angled tweezers to tweak and curve the stamens slightly to give more movement.

13 Dilute some black petal dust with clear alcohol and add a touch of white petal dust, too. Paint the tips of the stamens using a fine paintbrush. Leave to dry and then tinge the tips with a little dry sunflower yellow petal dust.

ASSEMBLY

14 Tape two small petals opposite each other onto the base of the stamens, using half-width nile green florist tape. It helps if the gum paste is still pliable at this stage, so that you can reshape the petals and create a more realistic effect. Next, tape two lager petals behind the small petals to cover the gaps, using half-width nile green florist tape.

15 Steam the flower (see page 32) to set the color and give a slight shine.

BUD

16 Tape over a 22-gauge wire with half-width nile green florist tape. Bend a hook in the end of the wire, using needle-nose pliers. Form a ball of pale green flower paste into an oval shape and insert the hooked wire into one end. Pinch the paste around the wire to neaten the connection and secure the two together.

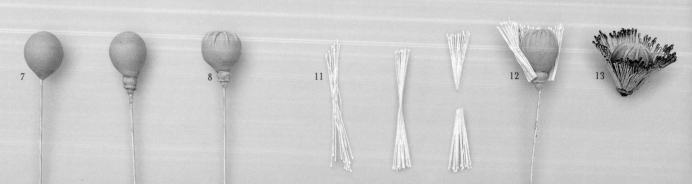

17 Use the plain-edge cutting wheel to divide the bud into two or three sections. Use a scriber or texturing wire brush to create gentle indents in the surface of the bud.

18 Use needle-nose pliers to bend the stem of the poppy bud into its characteristic nodding position. Allow to dry.

19 Dust the bud and the stem with a mixture of foliage green, forest green, and white petal dusts. Add a tinge of eggplant to the tip and the base of the bud. Spray very lightly with edible spray varnish or dip into a quarter-confectionery glaze.

LEAF

20 Roll out some well-kneaded pale green gum paste, leaving a thick ridge for the wire. Cut out the leaf using a poppy or coleus leaf cutter or the template on page 169 and an X-acto knife.

21 Insert a moistened 28- or 26-gauge wire into the thick ridge to support about half the length of the leaf. Place the leaf back on a nonstick board and use a rolling pin to broaden the shape a little.

22 Use the broad end of the dresden veining tool to work the edges of the serrated edge of the leaf to thin them out and add extra serrations at the same time.

23 Place the leaf into a double-sided cyclamen or thistle leaf veiner to texture the surface. Remove from the veiner and pinch the leaf from the base through to the tip to accentuate the central vein. Pinch the serrated sections between your finger and thumb to give a sharper effect. Allow to firm up before coloring.

24 Mix together foliage green, a touch of forest green, and white petal dust. Dust the front and back of the leaf. Add a tinge of eggplant petal dust to the edges.

ASSEMBLY

25 Tape a bud onto a 20-gauge wire, using half-width nile green florist tape. Next, tape a small leaf where the bud stem joins the main stem. Continue adding as many buds and leaves as required, followed by the flowers (which also have a leaf where the flower stem meets the main stem). Dust the stems with the same petal dust mixture used for the buds and leaves.

Petal dust locater

Stamen tips
Black and white mix

Sunflower

Petals
Eggplant (base)

Petals
Plum, African violet, and white mix

Ovary
Vine green, daffodil, and white mix

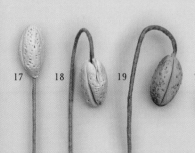

17   18   19

23   24

Flamingo Flower

This basic method of cutting petals with scissors and then shaping them with your fingers can be adopted to create many types of flowers. The flower shown here is a fantasy blossom that can be used as a filler flower in sprays and bouquets.

SKILL LEVEL ✿

Materials

- 28- and 24-gauge white wires
- Pink and pale green gum paste
- Corn starch (optional)
- Edible gum glue
- Stamens (as desired)
- Nile green florist tape
- Plum, eggplant, sunflower yellow, foliage green, and vine green petal dusts
- Half-confectionery glaze (see page 32) or edible glaze spray

Equipment

- Wire cutters or florist's scissors
- Nonstick pointed modeling tool, smooth pointed ceramic tool, or dowel
- Fine sharp scissors
- Foam pad
- Ball tool or bone end tool
- Tweezers
- Dusting brushes
- Nonstick board
- Double-sided rose leaf veiner

Hollow out the center of the teardrop (2).

PETALS

1 Cut several 28-gauge white wires into thirds using wire cutters or florist's scissors. Decide if you want to color the gum paste to a base color or leave it white. Here, the gum paste has been colored pale pink using plum petal dust (see page 30). Take a small ball of well-kneaded gum paste and form it into a teardrop shape using your finger and thumb.

2 Next, hollow out the broad end of the teardrop using the pointed end of the nonstick pointed modeling tool, smooth pointed ceramic tool, or a sharpened dowel.

3 Carefully cut the required number of petals with fine scissors—here, five even-sized petals have been created.

Cut five petals (3).

4 Open up the petals and then pinch each into a slightly pointed shape using your finger and thumb. Next, flatten and "pull" each petal slightly to thin it out—you might need a little corn starch on your finger and thumb if the gum paste feels sticky.

5 Place the flower face side on a firm foam pad or on your hand and thin out and hollow the back of each petal slightly, using a ball tool or bone end tool.

6 Moisten the wire with edible gum glue and thread it through the center of the flower, so that the tip of the wire is buried.

Pinch each petal into a point (4).

7 Use your finger and thumb to roll and thin out the back of the flower, creating a slender neck shape. Pinch off any excess length that is created in the process to create your desired effect. Flick and move the petals around a little to give some movement.

8 Stamens may be added to the center of the flower to add more detail/interest. Fold three stamens in half and trim away the excess length. You will now have six short stamens. Use tweezers to insert them into the center of the flower.

BUDS

9 Cut several short lengths of 28-gauge white wire. Take a small ball of well-kneaded pink gum paste and form it into a teardrop shape. Insert a wire into the broad end of the shape.

10 Use your finger and thumb to work the base of the cone shape down the wire to create a fine, long tapered neck.

11 Use tweezers or your fingers to pinch out three petals from the upper part of the bud shape. Thin each section between your finger and thumb.

12 Twist the petals back on themselves to create a spiral effect. Repeat to make buds in varying sizes.

13 Use quarter-width nile green florist tape to tape over each flower and bud stem.

COLORING

14 Dust the tips of the stamens with sunflower yellow petal dust. Use plum petal dust to color the petals and the long neck of the flower. Add tinges of eggplant at the base of the flower and at the tips.

LEAVES

15 Form a long, fine teardrop of pale green gum paste and insert a 28-gauge wire into the broad end, so that it supports at least half the length of the shape.

16 Place it against the nonstick board and use the flat side of the double-sided rose leaf veiner to flatten and thin out the shape.

Line up the tip and the base of the leaf with the central vein of the veiner (18).

17 Place the leaf on your palm or on a firm foam pad and thin out the edges using the ball tool. Work the tool half on the gum paste and half on your palm/pad.

18 Next place the leaf in the double-sided rose leaf veiner, lining up the tip and the base of the leaf with the central vein of the veiner. Press the top half of the veiner on top to give a firm imprint of the leaf texture.

Pinch to accentuate the central vein (19).

19 Remove the leaf from the veiner and pinch it from the base through to the tip to accentuate the central vein and curve the tip slightly. Repeat to make two more leaves to position on either side of the larger central leaf. Repeat to make leaf groups in varying sizes.

9   10   11   12   13   14   15   16

20 Color the leaves as desired. Here they have been dusted in layers starting with foliage green, and then over-dusted with vine green petal dusts. Tinge the edges with a mixture of plum and eggplant. Dip into a half-confectionery glaze or spray with edible glaze spray.

21 Tape each leaf stem/wire using quarter-width nile green florist tape and then tape the two smaller leaves on either side of a large leaf.

ASSEMBLY

22 Use half-width nile green florist tape to attach a small bud onto the end of a 24-gauge white wire. Add buds in graduating sizes down the wire and then introduce some flowers; alternate buds and flowers down the stem. Add groups of leaves at regular intervals down the stem. Dust the stem with a little of the plum and eggplant petal dust mixture.

Petal dust locater

Stamen tips
Sunflower yellow

Flower
Plum

Eggplant (base and tips)

Leaves
Plum and eggplant mix (edges)

Layers of foliage green and vine green

Stem
Plum and eggplant mix (edges)

18   19   20   21

Orchid

This very quick and effective orchid is made using a rose petal cutter and rose calyx cutter. It makes a useful addition as a secondary filler flower in a bouquet or spray or as an individual flower on mini cakes or even perhaps unwired on cupcakes. The final dusting and detail painting is entirely up to you, as this is a fantasy orchid.

SKILL LEVEL ❀

Materials

- White and mid-green gum paste
- 26- and 24-gauge white wires
- Edible gum glue
- Pieces of sponge or cotton ball
- Sunflower yellow, African violet, plum, white, vine green, eggplant, and foliage green petal dusts
- Clear alcohol
- Half-confectionery glaze (see page 32) or edible glaze spray
- Nile green florist tape

Equipment

- Nonstick board
- Nonstick rolling pin
- Small rose petal cutter or templates on page 171
- X-acto knife (optional)
- Dresden veining tool
- Amaryllis petal veiner or similar
- Ceramic silk veining tool or short wooden skewer
- Nonstick or ceramic modeling tool
- Rose calyx cutter
- Foam pad
- Ball tool
- Dusting brushes and fine paintbrush
- Double-sided amaryllis petal veiner

THROAT

1 As this is a quick orchid, it has no central column—only a throat petal that spirals back on itself, giving the illusion that the column is hidden deep in the throat. Roll out some well-kneaded white gum paste, leaving a thick ridge for the wire (see page 22). Cut out the throat petal using the small rose petal cutter or the petal template on page 171 and an X-acto knife. Insert a 26-gauge white wire moistened with edible gum glue into the thick ridge to support about half the length of the petal.

2 Work the base of the petal down onto the wire, using your finger and thumb in a rolling action. This will secure the wire and petal together and also create an elongated neck.

Frill the edges with the dresden veining tool (3).

3 Place the petal back against the nonstick board and use the broad end of the dresden veining tool "pull out" the edges of the petal at intervals to form a tight, frilled effect. Next, place the petal into the amaryllis petal veiner and press both sides together firmly to texture the surface.

4 Use the ceramic silk veining tool or a short wooden skewer to frill the edges a little more to create a softer effect.

5 Finally, curl the base of the petal back onto itself to create a trumpet shape. Curl the edges of the rest of the petal back slightly. Use the dresden veining tool to open up the curled base to create a deeper throat effect. Leave to dry a little.

OUTER PETALS

6 The outer petals are made from a rose calyx shape as an all-in-one flower, speeding up the flower production a little. Form a ball of well-kneaded white gum paste into a cone shape. Pinch out the broad end of the cone to form a "hat" shape. Place the "brim" of the hat on the nonstick board and thin it out using the nonstick or ceramic modeling tool.

7 Cut out the flower shape using a rose calyx cutter or the template on page 171 and an X-acto knife, positioning the thicker central node in the center of the cutter. Remove the shape from the cutter and place it flat side down on the board.

1 2 3 4 5 6

7

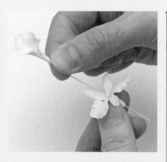

Hollow out the "head" petal with the ball tool (10).

Draw a central vein on the backs of the "arm" petals (11).

Thread the wired throat petal through the center of the outer petals (12).

Apply sunflower yellow petal dust deep into the throat petal (13).

8 If you now imagine this shape as a figure, you need to broaden the arms using the nonstick modeling tool or ceramic silk veining tool. Leave a slight ridge down the center of these two petals.

9 Use the dresden veining tool to pull/work the edges as created for the throat petal. Next, rest the flower against your index finger and frill the edges to create a softer effect, using the ceramic silk veining tool.

10 Place the shape on a firm foam pad or on your palm and soften the edges of the other three petals using the ball tool. Use the same tool to hollow out the "head" petal so that it curves forward and the backs of the "leg" petals so that they curve backward.

11 Use the fine end of the dresden veining tool to draw a central vein on the backs of the frilled "arm" petals. Pinch the tips of each of the five petals with your finger and thumb to create more pointed petal shapes. Use the pointed end of the nonstick or ceramic modeling tool to open it up slightly.

12 Next, moisten the center with a little edible gum glue and then thread the wired throat petal through the center. Position the head petal so that it curves over in the direction of the throat petal. Work the gum paste at the back of the flower between your finger and thumb to secure the throat and outer petals together and also to create a finer tapered neck. Pinch off any excess gum paste from the base. Reposition the two "arm" petals forward slightly. You might need to support the petals with pieces of sponge or cotton ball until they dry a little.

COLORING

13 Use a small brush to apply sunflower yellow petal dust deep in the throat. Tinge the edges of the throat using a mixture of African violet and plum petal dusts, then use the same mixture to catch the outer petals very gently, too. Use white and vine green petal dusts mixed together to tinge the back of the orchid and the very tips of the outer petals, and also at the base of the petals where the throat petal joins the flower.

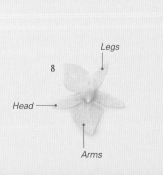

8

Legs

Head

Arms

9

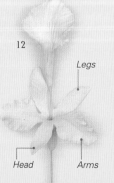

12

Legs

Head

Arms

14

Paint a series of fine lines inside the throat (14).

14 Dilute a small amount of eggplant petal dust with clear alcohol and paint a series of fine lines radiating from deep inside the orchid throat. Tape over each of the flower stems with half-width nile green florist tape.

LEAVES

15 Form a long teardrop shape of well-kneaded mid-green gum paste and insert a 26-gauge white wire to support the whole length.

16 Work the gum paste between your finger and thumb to elongate the shape.

17 Place it on the nonstick board and use the flat side of the amaryllis petal veiner to flatten the shape.

18 Soften the edges using the ball tool, then place the shape in the double-sided amaryllis petal veiner to texture the surface.

19 Remove the leaf from the veiner and then pinch it from the base through to the tip to accentuate a central vein and curve the leaf.

20 Dust in layers, starting with foliage green and then overdust with vine green. Add a gentle tinge of eggplant to the edges. Leave to dry, then dip into a half-confectionery glaze or spray lightly with edible glaze spray.

ASSEMBLY

21 Tape the flowers onto a 24-gauge wire using half-width nile green florist tape, alternating the flowers down either side of the stem. Add a pair of leaves to the base of the stem.

Petal dust locater

Flowers
Sunflower yellow (inside throat)

Eggplant (painted detail)

White and green mix (back of flower, tips of petals, outside base of throat)

African violet and plum mix (edges of petals)

Leaves
Layers of foliage green and vine green

Eggplant (edges)

15 16 17 18 19 20

Anemone

Translated from the Greek, the name
Anemone means "daughter of the wind,"
giving rise to its other popular name of
wind flower. Anemones are native to
Mediterranean countries and also parts of
Asia. The flowers may be white, green,
cream, pink, blue, purple, red, cerise, or
a dark burgundy, with the stamens being
very dark or creamy green or yellow.

SKILL LEVEL ❀ ❀

Materials

- 28-, 26-, and 22-gauge white wires
- Pale green and white gum paste
- Edible gum glue
- Pollen powder
- Black, deep purple, plum, African violet, eggplant, foliage green, and vine green petal dusts
- White seed-head stamens
- Hi-tack nontoxic craft glue
- Clear alcohol
- Pale green or white florist tape
- Quarter-confectionery glaze (see page 32) or edible glaze spray

Equipment

- Needle-nose pliers
- Fine curved scissors
- Sharp scissors
- Dresden veining tool or small palette knife
- Dusting brushes
- Fine paintbrush
- Nonstick rolling pin
- Anemone or rose petal cutters or templates on page 172
- X-acto knife
- Florist's scissors or wire cutters
- Ball tool
- Foam pad
- Anemone, poppy, or small hibiscus double-sided petal veiner
- Anemone leaf cutter (see page 172)
- Galax or wild geranium leaf veiner

Snip into the surface of the center to give texture (1).

Moisten the center with edible gum glue, then dip into colored pollen powder (2).

Stick groups of stamens together, then cut in half (3).

CENTER

1 Bend a hook in the end of a 22-gauge white wire using needle-nose pliers. Roll a ball of pale green gum paste and insert the hooked wire moistened with edible gum glue into it. Pinch the base of the ball against the wire to secure it. Use fine, curved scissors to snip gently into the surface of the paste to give a little texture.

2 Mix together pollen powder with black and deep purple petal dusts. Moisten the surface of the wired center with edible gum glue and dip it into the pollen powder to cover the surface evenly. Leave to dry.

3 Take about half a bunch of white seed-head stamens and divide it into smaller groups, lining up their tips. Use hi-tack nontoxic craft glue to bond each group together, working from the center toward the tips at both ends. Leave a small length of stamen unglued at either end, making sure that the line of glue is even. Try not to use too much glue, as this will slow down the drying process. Next, cut the stamen groups in half using sharp scissors and trim each set of stamens shorter. It is best to position a group next to the center to decide just how long they need to be.

4 Use white gum paste and edible gum glue mashed together using the dresden veining tool or a small palette knife to create a sticky, almost chewing-gum-consistency glue. Use this glue to attach the sets of stamens evenly around the wired center. Hold each group to the count of 10—this is usually enough time for the stamens to bond well. Leave to dry.

5 Dust the stamens with plum petal dust. The stamens usually correspond with the color of the flower. Next, dilute some black petal dust with a touch of African violet with clear alcohol. Use a fine paintbrush to paint the tips of the stamens, making sure that there are no white tips remaining. Leave to dry.

1

2

4

5

Use half-width florist tape to secure the petals together (10).

PETALS

6 The number of petals varies between varieties of anemone. There can be as few as five petals, although mostly there are more. Roll out some well-kneaded white gum paste, leaving a thick ridge for the wire. Cut out a petal shoe using an anemone or rose petal cutter or the template on page 172 and an X-acto knife.

7 Cut several lengths of 28-gauge white wire into thirds, using florist's scissors or wire cutters. Moisten the end of a wire with edible gum glue and insert it into the thick ridge of the petal to support about one-third to half of the length.

8 Use the ball tool to soften the edge of the petal against your palm or a firm foam pad. Place the petal into an anemone, poppy or small hibiscus double-sided petal veiner and press firmly to texture it. Remove from the veiner and hollow the center gently using your fingers and thumb. Repeat to make the required number of petals. You might decide to use all the same size petals or increase the size very slightly for some of the petals—this very much depends on the variety you are making.

COLORING

9 If you intend to create a strongly colored flower, it is best to dust the petals while they are still pliable so that the color can be scrubbed evenly into the surface. Here, plum petal dust has been used to color the petals. Dust the upper surface strongly, leaving a small area at the base of each petal white and much lighter on the back.

ASSEMBLY

10 Use half-width pale green or white florist tape to secure the petals around the stamen center. If you have made petals in graduating sizes, start with the smaller petals. It is best to vary the numbers of petals with each flower to give a more interesting finished display on a cake. Leave to dry and then hold over the steam from a just-boiled kettle or use a clothes steamer to set the color and take away the dusty finish left by the petal dust (see page 32).

LEAVES

11 You will need to make three or four leaves for each flower. Roll out some well-kneaded pale green gum paste, leaving a thick ridge for the wire—it is best to do this by hand instead of using a grooved board, as a slightly thicker ridge is required than used for the petals. Use the anemone leaf cutter or the leaf template on page 172 and an X-acto knife. Cut a length of 26-gauge white wire into thirds. Moisten the end of a wire with edible gum glue and insert it into the thick ridge of the leaf. The leaf is quite fragile in shape, so you will need to make sure the wire supports most of the length of the central section.

12 Use the galax or wild geranium leaf veiner to texture the surface of the leaf.

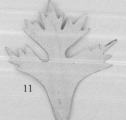

6　7　8　9　10　11

Thin the edges of the leaves with the dresden veining tool (13).

13 Use the broad end of the dresden veining tool to thin out the leaf sections at intervals to create a more fringed effect. Use fine scissors to remove tiny "V"-shaped cuts from the edge of the leaf. Pinch the leaf from the base through to the tip and curve back the leaf slightly. Repeat to make three leaves.

COLORING

14 Dust the edges of each leaf with a mixture of eggplant and plum petal dusts. For a purple flower, use African violet instead of plum. Use foliage green to dust each leaf from the base fading through to the tips.

Pinch from tip to base to emphasize the central vein (13).

Overdust with vine green petal dust, taking care not to damage the fine cut edge. Dip into a quarter-confectionery glaze or spray lightly with edible glaze spray. Leave the glaze to dry.

ASSEMBLY

15 Tape the three leaves directly onto the flower stem, using half-width pale green or white florist tape. Dust the stem gently with a mixture of vine green and foliage green petal dusts. Tinge with eggplant petal dust.

12

14

Petal dust locater

Stamens
Black and African violet mix (tips)

Plum

Seed head
Black and deep purple mix

Petals
Plum

Leaves
Layers of foliage green and vine green

Eggplant and plum mix (edges)

Plum (edges)

Chinese Lanterns

Physalis alkekengi—more affectionately known as Chinese lanterns—are native to China, Japan, and Korea. They are prized by florists for use in autumnal arrangements and displays and make a great addition to Halloween cakes. Florists often strip the foliage from the stems to make the lanterns stand out in a more dramatic fashion. They also look very effective sprayed gold or silver for use on Christmas cakes. The lanterns look best made in graduating sizes. The small lanterns are very green, ripening through to orange and orange-red as the season progresses and the lanterns mature. They can be made with pale green gum paste and pale orange gum paste, but more graduation and a brighter effect can be achieved by making the lanterns with very pale yellow gum paste and then dusting them with layers of graduating color afterward.

SKILL LEVEL ❀ ❀ ❀

Materials

- Pale yellow and pale green gum paste
- 28-, 26-, 24- and 22-gauge white wires
- Edible gum glue
- White and nile green florist tape
- Vine green, foliage green, tangerine, coral, ruby, and eggplant petal dusts
- Edible glaze spray

Equipment

- Nonstick board
- Nonstick modeling tool or smooth ceramic tool
- Large rose calyx cutters or templates on page 172
- X-acto knife
- Physalis or clematis leaf veiner
- Angled tweezers
- Needle-nose pliers
- Tea light
- Polystyrene dummy cake (or similar)
- Fine paintbrush
- Fine scissors
- Dusting brushes
- Nonstick modeling tool or ceramic silk veining tool
- Plain-edge cutting wheel
- Dresden veining tool
- Foam pad
- Ball tool

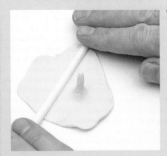

Do not roll the brim of the hat too thinly (1).

LANTERNS

1 Take a large ball of well-kneaded pale yellow gum paste and form it into a cone shape. Pinch the broad end of the shape to form a hat shape. Place the "brim" of the hat on the nonstick board and roll out the brim, using a nonstick modeling tool or smooth ceramic tool. Do not roll the paste too thinly at this stage.

2 Cut out the lantern, using a large rose calyx cutter or the template on page 172 and an X-acto knife. Remove the shape from the cutter and place it flat on the nonstick board.

Use the large rose calyx cutter for the lanterns (2).

3 Next, broaden each of the sepals using the nonstick modeling tool or smooth ceramic tool. Try to leave a thick ridge running down the center of each sepal, as this will give more support to the piece. Now use the same tool to elongate each sepal. This process creates a larger lantern and also thins out each of the sepals.

4 Vein each of the five sepals using the physalis or clematis leaf veiner. You need the veins to be raised on the outer surface of the lantern—this is done using the back of the leaf veiner. Use angled tweezers to extend the ridges into the center of the shape.

Heat the hooked end of the wire before embedding it into the center (5).

5 Use needle-nose pliers to bend a large open hook in the end of a 24- or 22-gauge white wire. Thread the unhooked end of the wire through the raised center of the lantern, but don't embed the hook just yet. Now heat the hooked end of the wire in the tea light until it is red hot. Quickly and very carefully embed the hot hook into the center of the lantern, taking care not to burn yourself with the hot sugar. The sugar will caramelize and set quickly. This gives a stronger bond than using edible gum glue at this stage, which can make the lantern slide off the wire.

2

3

4

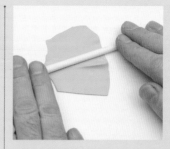

Trim the ridges left after pinching the sides together with fine scissors (8).

Drag petal dust over the raised veins (9).

Leave a ridge for the wire (10).

Vein using a physalis or clematis leaf veiner (11).

6 Insert the other end of the wire into a polystyrene dummy cake—this will give you both hands free to join the sepals together into the lantern shape. Use a fine paintbrush to paint the edges of each sepal with edible gum glue. Join two sepals together and then join the opposite two sepals together. Stick the two sets together, which leaves the single sepal to be tucked into the group carefully.

7 Pinch the edges of the sepals to create a good, tight connection.

8 There will be ridges created from pinching the sections together. To remove these, simply trim them with fine scissors. Tape over the stem with quarter-width white florist tape. Repeat to make lanterns in graduating sizes.

COLORING

9 Dust the smaller lanterns with a mixture of vine green and foliage green petal dusts. Add tinges of tangerine. Dust the larger lanterns and their stems heavily with tangerine petal dust and then coral followed by ruby. Use the flat of the brush to drag against the raised veins of the lanterns to highlight the veining. Leave to dry and then spray lightly with edible glaze spray. Use needle-nose pliers to bend each of the stems.

LEAVES

10 Roll out some pale green gum paste using the nonstick modeling tool or ceramic silk veining tool, leaving a thick ridge for the wire. Insert a 28- or 26-gauge white wire moistened with edible gum glue into the ridge.

11 Place the wired paste into the physalis or clematis leaf veiner and press firmly to texture the leaf.

12 Remove the paste from the veiner and trim around the edge using the plain-edge cutting wheel, an X-acto knife, or fine scissors.

Here, a plain-edge cutting wheel is used to trim the leaf (12).

Create a serrated edge with the dresden veining tool (13).

6

7

9

Tangerine
petal dust

Ruby petal dust

12

Dust the edges of the leaf with eggplant petal dust (14).

13 Place the leaf on the nonstick board and work the edges at intervals with the broad end of the dresden veining tool to create a slightly serrated edge. Place the leaf on the firm foam pad or the palm of your hand and soften the edges with the ball tool. Pinch the leaf from the base to the tip to accentuate the central vein. Repeat to make leaves in varying sizes.

14 Dust the leaves to the very edges in layers of vine green, foliage green, and tinges of eggplant petal dusts. Spray very lightly with edible glaze spray.

ASSEMBLY

15 Tape two small leaves to the end of a 22-gauge white wire, using half-width nile green florist tape. Continue adding the leaves in pairs down the stem, accompanied by a small green lantern. Gradually introduce the larger orange lanterns. Add extra 22-gauge white wire as you work down the stem to give extra support. Dust the stem with vine green, foliage green, and tinges of eggplant petal dusts. Spray the stem lightly with edible glaze spray to seal the color. Leave to dry. Use needle-nose pliers to bend and curve the main stem a little.

Petal dust locater

Lanterns (small)
Vine green and
foliage green mix

Tangerine

Leaves
Layers of vine green
and foliage green

Eggplant (edges)

Lanterns (large)
Layers of tangerine,
coral, and ruby

13   14   15

Clown Orchid

Rossioglossum orchids—often known as clown orchids— are part of a
small group of orchid species from Central America. The
brightly colored yellow and red flowers have a slightly clown-like
appearance and add instant warmth and a sense of the exotic to
any floral display. The flower pictured here has been simplified
slightly to make it more accessible for general cake decorating.

SKILL LEVEL ❀ ❀ ❀

Materials

- Pale sunflower yellow and white gum paste
- Sunflower yellow, ruby, coral, and eggplant petal dusts
- 28- and 26-gauge white wires
- Edible gum glue
- Clear alcohol
- Nile green florist tape
- Foam pad
- Edible glaze spray (optional)

Equipment

- Ceramic silk veining tool
- X-acto knife
- Nonstick board
- Nonstick rolling pin
- Clown orchid cutters or templates on page 171
- Dresden veining tool
- Double-sided stargazer B petal veiner
- Paper towel or aluminum foil
- Tiny plunger blossom cutter
- Smooth ceramic tool
- Dusting brushes
- Fine paintbrush
- Wire cutters or florist's scissors
- Foam pad (optional)
- Ball tool
- Plain-edge cutting wheel

COLUMN

1 Attach a tiny ball of pale sunflower yellow gum paste onto the end of a 28-gauge white wire. Work the paste down the wire slightly to create a slender teardrop shape. Hollow out the underside by simply placing the shape against the top curved area of the ceramic silk veining tool. Press the column against the tool using your finger and thumb, which will also create a slight ridge at the back of the column. Leave to dry.

2 Attach a tiny ball of white gum paste to the top edge of the column. Divide it into two sections using the X-acto knife. This represents the anther cap.

LABELLUM

3 Roll out some well-kneaded pale sunflower yellow gum paste, leaving a thick ridge for the wire. The orchid is quite fleshy, so don't roll the paste too fine. Cut out the labellum shape using the rounded cutter from the clown orchid set or the template on page 171 and an X-acto knife.

The anther cap is made from a tiny ball of gum paste (2).

4 Insert a 26-gauge white wire moistened with edible gum glue carefully into the fine section of the petal shape and gradually through into the main rounded section to give it maximum support. Use the broad end of the dresden veining tool to flatten and thin out the two small sections at the base of the petal.

5 Place the petal into the double-sided stargazer B petal veiner and press firmly to texture the petal. Remove from the veiner and rest the petal against your index finger. Use the ceramic silk veining tool at intervals around the edge of the rounded section of the petal to frill and texture it slightly.

Pinch back the bottom of the rounded section (6).

6 Next, use your finger and thumb to pinch back the bottom of the rounded section to create a "waistline." Pinch the tip of the rounded section from behind to give a little movement. Leave to firm up over crumpled paper towel or aluminum foil.

7 There is a raised platform on the labellum. The method used here is not botanically correct, but it creates a quicker and more pleasing finish to the eye. Roll out some pale sunflower yellow gum paste, not too thinly. Cut out a blossom shape using the tiny plunger blossom cutter. Use the pointed end of the smooth ceramic tool to hollow out the center of the blossom. Attach to the labellum using edible gum glue.

1

4

5

7

Tape the column to the labellum (9).

COLORING

8 Dust the petal from the base fading to the edges using sunflower yellow petal dust. Bring some of the color in from the edges, too. Next, add some detail spots with a fine paintbrush, using ruby petal dust diluted with clear alcohol. Leave to dry and then catch the edges of the petal with coral and ruby petal dusts.

9 Tape the column onto the base of the labellum, using quarter-width nile green florist tape, placing the hollowed side down toward the petal. Dust the column with sunflower yellow petal dust and catch the edges with the coral/ruby mixture.

PETALS

10 Roll out some well-kneaded pale sunflower yellow gum paste, leaving a thick ridge for the wire. Cut out the petal shape, using the wide side petal cutter from the clown orchid set or the template on page 171 and an X-acto knife. Cut a length of 26-gauge white wire into thirds, using wire cutters or florist's scissors. Moisten the end of a wire with edible gum glue and insert it into the thick ridge of the petal to support about half the length of the petal.

11 Place the petal on a firm foam pad or the palm of your hand and use the ball tool to soften the edge, working half on the edge of the petal and half on your pad/hand. Next, texture the petal using the double-sided stargazer B petal veiner. Press firmly to create strong veining. Frill the edges of the petal using the ceramic silk veining tool, resting the petal against your index finger and working at intervals to create a little movement. Next, pinch the tip of the petal into a point and then pinch the base of the petal back slightly. Repeat to make a second petal. Leave to firm up a little (but not dry) before coloring.

SEPALS

12 Roll out some well-kneaded pale sunflower yellow gum paste, leaving a thick ridge for the wire. Cut out the sepal shape, using the narrowest cutter from the clown orchid set or the template on page 171 and a plain-edge cutting wheel or X-acto knife. Moisten the end of a 26-gauge white wire with edible gum glue and insert it into the thick ridge of the sepal to support about half its length. Place the sepal on the firm foam pad or palm of your hand and soften the edge gently, using the ball tool.

13 Texture the sepal using the double-sided stargazer B petal veiner. Remove from the veiner and pinch the sepal from the base through to the tip to create a gentle central vein. Curve the petal backward and leave to firm up a little. This will be the dorsal sepal that sits almost like a head to the flower. Repeat the process to make two more sepals, allowing them to dry in a curved formation, rather like legs.

8

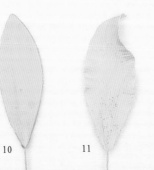

10   11   12

13

14

Dilute ruby petal dust with clear alcohol to create the paint for the detail (14).

COLORING AND ASSEMBLY

14 Dust the petals and sepals using sunflower petal dust. Catch the edges with a mixture of coral and ruby petal dusts. Add detail spots of varying sizes to the petals using ruby petal dust diluted with clear alcohol. Create stronger, almost striped markings on the narrower sepals.

15 Use half-width nile green florist tape to position and tape two petals onto either side of the labellum. Then tape the third petal coming up behind the labellum. If the gum paste is still pliable this is good, as it will allow you to reshape the petals a little to give more movement to the flower.

16 Next, tape in the narrow dorsal (head) sepal, followed by the two lateral (leg) sepals. Use a mixture of eggplant and ruby petal dusts to add tinges of color to the back of the outer sepals. Leave the flower to dry and then either hold over the steam from a just-boiled kettle (see page 32) or spray lightly with edible glaze spray to seal the color and give a slightly waxy finish.

Petal dust locater

Labellum, petals, and sepals

Sunflower yellow

Coral and ruby mix (edges)

Ruby (details)

Eggplant and ruby (back)

Column
Sunflower yellow

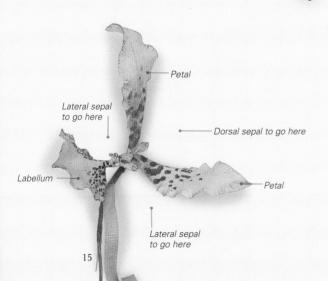

Petal

Lateral sepal to go here

Dorsal sepal to go here

Labellum

Petal

Lateral sepal to go here

15

Gardenia

Exotic gardenias, prized by florists for their exquisite heavy perfume, are often used for bridal bouquets and corsages. There are hundreds of species of gardenia, varying in size and number of petals. The flowers are mostly white and cream, but there are yellow and orange forms, too. The instructions here outline how to make a gardenia with a tight, spiraled center and also an open center.

SKILL LEVEL ❀ ❀ ❀

Materials

- 33-, 30-, 28-, 26-, 24- and 22-gauge white wires
- White, pale green and mid-green gum paste
- Edible gum glue
- White seed-head stamens
- Nile green and white florist tape
- Sunflower yellow, vine green, white, foliage green, woodland green, forest green, and eggplant petal dusts
- Clear alcohol
- Three-quarter-confectionery glaze (see page 32) or edible glaze spray

Equipment

- Needle-nose pliers
- Nonstick rolling pin
- Nonstick board
- Christmas rose or gardenia cutters (or see templates on page 173)
- X-acto knife
- Metal ball tool
- Double-sided rose petal veiner or Christmas rose petal veiner
- Foam pad
- Dresden veining tool
- Fine tweezers and flat-edged angled tweezers
- Dusting brushes
- Grooved board (optional)
- Wire cutters or sharp florist's scissors
- Sharp fine scissors
- Plain-edge cutting wheel (optional)
- Orchid wing petal cutter (optional)
- Gardenia leaf veiner

SPIRALED TIGHT CENTER

1 Bend a hook in the end of a 24-gauge white wire using needle-nose pliers. Take a small ball of well-kneaded white gum paste and form it into a cone shape. Moisten the hook with a tiny amount of edible gum glue and insert it into the broad base of the cone. This cone needs to be really quite small in comparison with the smallest of the petal cutters being used. Leave to dry overnight.

2 Roll out some well-kneaded white gum paste not too thinly on a nonstick board and cut out six small petals, using either the smallest Christmas rose or gardenia cutter, or the template on page 173 and an X-acto knife.

Texture each petal using a double-sided veiner (3A).

3 Use the metal ball tool to soften the edges slightly and then texture each petal in turn, using either the rose petal veiner, which creates a slightly deeper veining (as used here), or the rose or Christmas rose petal veiner.

4 Place the petal on a firm foam pad or the palm of your hand and use the broad end of the dresden veining tool to work on the inside edge on the left-hand side of each petal to create a curled edge.

Attach the first petal onto the wired cone (5A).

5 Moisten the dried cone with a little edible gum glue. Place the first petal against the cone, pressing the uncurled edge tightly toward the tip of the cone.

6 Continue adding the petals one by one to create a tight spiral. Curl back the curled edges a little as you go and tuck the last petal edge under the first one. Set to one side while you make the outer wired petals.

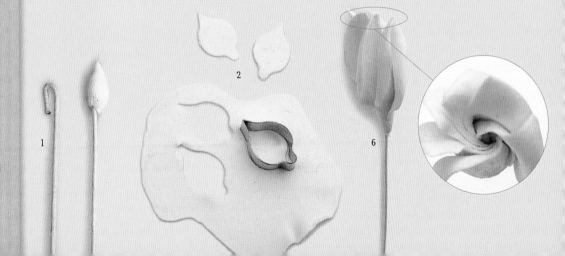

ALTERNATIVE OPEN CENTER

If you decide to create a more open flower, then you will need first of all to create a stamen and pistil center.

1 Use a 28-gauge white wire for the pistil. Form a tiny cone shape of pale green gum paste and insert the wire into the broad end. Thin the paste down the wire to form an almost bud shape. Use fine tweezers to pinch three fine ridges into the sides of the shape. Twist the pinched sections around to form a fine point. Leave to dry.

2 Tape six white seed-head stamens around the base of the pistil, using quarter-width nile green florist tape. Dust the tips gently with sunflower yellow petal dust.

3 Roll some well-kneaded white gum paste, leaving a thick ridge (a grooved board may also be used). Cut out a petal, lining

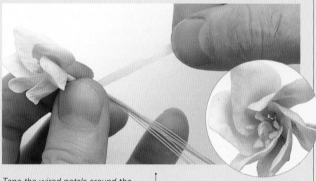

Tape the wired petals around the pistil in a spiral formation (5).

up the ridge down the length of the smallest Christmas rose/ gardenia cutter, or use an X-acto knife and the template on page 173. Moisten the end of a 30-gauge white wire with edible gum glue and insert it into the thick ridge to support one-third to half the length of the petal, pinching the base of the petal onto the wire to make sure it is secured well. Repeat to make six petals.

4 Soften the edge of the petal, then vein and curl back the left-hand edge as described in Steps 3 and 4 on page 113. Repeat to make six petals. Cup the center of each petal very gently using the metal ball tool.

5 Use quarter-width white florist tape to tape the six petals around the pistil and stamens, creating a spiraled shape.

OUTER PETALS

7 Roll out a piece of well-kneaded white gum paste, leaving a thick ridge for the wire (a grooved board may be used). Cut out the petal using the second size of Christmas rose/ gardenia cutter or the template on page 173 and an X-acto knife.

8 Insert a 30- or 28-gauge white wire moistened with edible gum glue into the thick ridge to support about one-third to half the length of the petal. Pinch the paste at the base of the petal onto the wire to secure it.

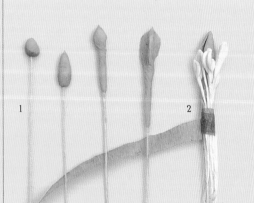

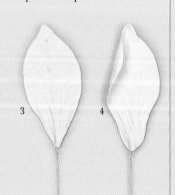

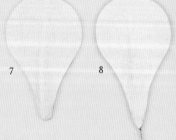

1

2

3

4

7

8

9 Place the petal on a firm foam pad or the palm of your hand and soften the edge using the metal ball tool, working half on the edge of the petal and half on the pad/palm. Next, texture the surface using a double-sided rose petal veiner or Christmas rose petal veiner. Remove the petal from the veiner and place back on the pad/palm.

10 Use the dresden veining tool to curl the left-hand edge of the back of the petal, as before. Repeat to make six petals. Pinch the tips slightly here and there, too.

ASSEMBLY

11 Tape the six petals around the tight or open center using quarter-width white florist tape, positioning each petal over a seam in the first layer. It is good at this stage if the paste is still slightly pliable, as this will enable you to pinch and re-curl some of the petals slightly to give a more relaxed finished flower.

12 Repeat the above process to make a full flower, creating six petals using the largest of the Christmas rose/gardenia petal cutters or the templates on page 173 and an X-acto knife. Leave the petals to firm up slightly, but do not let them dry completely before attaching to the flower. Tape each of the larger petals to cover seams in the second layer, using quarter-width white florist tape. If the petals are still pliable, you should be able to pinch and re-curl them for the previous layer to create more movement.

Create a neck from a ball of gum paste worked down the wire (13).

NECK

13 Attach a ball of white gum paste behind the back of the flower and work it between your finger down the wire to form a slender neck—the exact length varies between varieties. Use the broad end of the dresden veining tool and a little clear alcohol to blend the seam between the neck and the petals together. Take care not to use too much liquid, as this will dissolve the sugar.

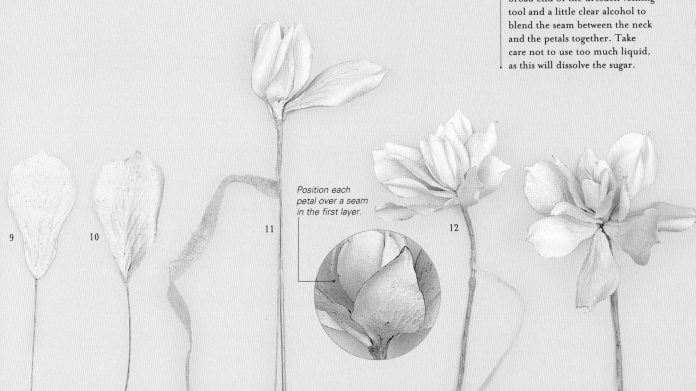

Position each petal over a seam in the first layer.

9   10   11   12

Dust a streak of nile green onto the back of each petal (14).

COLORING

14 Mix together vine green and white petal dusts. Dust the neck of the flower from the base, fading toward the back of the petals. Add a streak of the color to the underside of each curled back outer petal. Add more white petal dust to the mixture and add a gentle tinge of woodland green to the central petals. Some gardenias have a slight green tinge while others are more creamy. Leave the flower to dry and then hold it over the steam from a just-boiled kettle or use a clothes steamer (see page 32) to give the flower a waxy finish.

CALYX

15 Cut six short lengths of 33-gauge white wire using wire cutters or sharp florist's scissors. Attach a tiny ball of mid-green gum paste about 1 in. (2.5 cm) from the end of the wire.

16 Work and blend to extend the paste to the tip of the wire, removing any excess bulk to create a fine sepal shape. Place the sepal on the nonstick board and use the flat side of a leaf veiner to press the shape to flatten it.

17 Pinch the sepal from the base through to the tip to give it a central vein. Repeat to make six sepals. Dust with foliage green petal dust.

18 Tape the six sepals around the base of the neck of the flower, using quarter-width nile green florist tape. Curve them back slightly.

BUDS

19 Bend a hook in the end of a 22-gauge white wire using needle-nose pliers. Take a ball of well-kneaded white gum paste and form it into a cone shape. Moisten the hook with edible gum glue and insert it into the base of the cone. Use your finger and thumb to work the base of the cone down onto the wire to create a slender neck. Trim off any excess using sharp fine scissors.

20 Use flat-edged angled tweezers to pinch six fine flanges from the upper section of the bud to represent the outer petals. Next, use your finger and thumb to pinch each section more finely on the very edges. Now twist the petals back on themselves in a spire formation. The direction of petal flow varies between varieties.

21 Dust the base of the neck with a mixture of vine green and white petal dusts. Add a streak of the color to the grooves of each of the petals. Create and add a calyx, as described in steps 15–18.

LEAVES

22 Roll out some well-kneaded mid-green gum paste, leaving a thick ridge for the wire. Cut out the leaf shape, using either the plain-edge cutting wheel and the templates on page 173 or an orchid wing petal cutter. The leaves of the gardenia are quite waxy/fleshy, so do not roll the paste too fine.

23 Depending on the size of the leaf, insert a 28-, 26-, or 24-gauge white wire into the thick ridge of the leaf to support about half the length of the leaf.

15   16   17   18   19   20   21

Glaze with edible glaze spray or three-quarter-confectionery glaze (26).

Place the leaf on a firm foam pad or your palm and, using the metal ball tool, soften the edge slightly to take away the just-cut look.

24 Place the leaf into a double-sided gardenia leaf veiner and press the two sides together firmly to texture the leaf. Remove the leaf from the veiner and carefully pinch it from behind at the base, guiding through to the tip to accentuate the central vein. Some varieties of gardenia have hollowed-out backs to their foliage: simply hollow gently with the metal ball tool or your fingers and thumb.

COLORING

25 The new growth foliage is a brighter green than the older leaves. Again, different varieties have different depths of green. Here, the leaves are dusted in layers with woodland green, forest green, foliage green, and vine green petal dusts. Catch the edges very slightly with eggplant petal dust. It is often best to dust the foliage while the paste is still pliable, so that an intense color may be achieved.

26 Leave the leaves to dry before glazing. Spray with edible glaze spray or dip into a three-quarter-confectionery glaze.

ASSEMBLY

27 Tape the smaller leaves around the base of the buds and the flowers. Continue adding leaves as desired, increasing the size as you work.

Petal dust locater

Stamens
Sunflower yellow
(tips)

Petals
Vine green and white mix
(base, underside, center)

Leaves
Layers of woodland green,
forest green, foliage
green, and vine green

22   23   24   25

Pelargonium

Pelargoniums, often incorrectly known as geraniums, are native to South Africa. There are over 200 species of pelargonium and many more hybrid forms. The scented leaves and flowers are edible and are often used to flavor cakes, jellies, and desserts, making them an ideal subject to recreate in sugar.

SKILL LEVEL ✿ ✿

Materials

- Fine white cotton thread (optional)
- Hi-tack nontoxic craft glue (optional)
- Fine white stamens
- 30-, 28-, 26-, 24-, and 22-gauge white wires
- Coral, red, sunflower yellow, ruby, foliage green, vine green, forest green and eggplant petal dusts
- Pale coral and pale green gum paste
- Edible gum glue
- Nile green florist tape
- Corn starch
- Clear alcohol
- Edible glaze spray

Equipment

- Scissors
- Dusting brushes
- Nonstick board
- Nonstick rolling pin
- Grooved board (optional)
- Small rose petal cutters or template on page 171
- Nonstick modeling stick or smooth ceramic tool
- Double-sided soft hibiscus or rose petal veiner
- Small rose calyx cutter or template on page 171
- Dresden veining tool
- Needle-nose pliers
- Plain-edge cutting wheel or X-acto knife
- Pelargonium leaf cutters or templates on page 172
- Ball tool
- Double-sided pelargonium leaf veiner

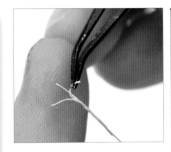

Curl back the tips of the pistil with angled tweezers (1).

PISTIL

1 Creating the pistil is optional, as it is a very fine part of the center. Using scissors, cut five lengths of fine white cotton thread. Use a tiny amount of hi-tack nontoxic craft glue to bond the lengths together, leaving the tips unglued. Leave to set and then curl back the tips. Trim off any excess length from the tips using scissors.

STAMENS

2 Take five fine white stamens and fold them in half to line up their tips. Use a tiny amount of hi-tack nontoxic craft glue to bond the stamens together, leaving a little of their length unglued. Leave to set for a few minutes and then trim off the excess bulk using sharp scissors.

Use coral and red petal dusts to color the pistil and sunflower to color the tips (3).

Attach the stamens and pistil to the end of a 30-gauge white wire using a little more of the hi-tack glue. Hold in place to the count of 10—this usually gives enough time for the two to bond together.

3 Dust the pistil with coral and red petal dusts. Catch the tips of the stamens with sunflower petal dust.

PETALS

4 Roll out some well-kneaded pale coral gum paste, leaving a thick ridge for the wire (as the petals are small, a grooved board may be used to speed up the process). Cut out a petal shape, using a small rose petal cutter or the template on page 171 and an X-acto knife.

5 Insert a 30- or 28-gauge white wire moistened with edible gum glue to support about half the length of the petal. Pinch the base of the petal against the wire and work it slightly onto the wire to create a short neck.

6 Next, use the nonstick modeling stick or smooth ceramic tool to broaden the petal slightly across the top half of the petal. The five petals are sometimes all the same size, while other varieties have three petals larger than the other two.

7 Texture the petal using the double-sided soft hibiscus or rose petal veiner. Pinch the petal from the base very gently to give a little shaping. Repeat the process to make five petals.

2

4

5

6

7

COLORING AND ASSEMBLY

8 Dust the upper surface of the petals heavily with a mixture of red and coral petal dusts. Add a tinge of ruby petal dust to the edge too.

9 Tape the five petals onto the stamens, using quarter-width nile green florist tape. Position two petals close together on one side of the flower and the other three together on the opposite side.

CALYX

10 Take a small ball of pale green gum paste and form into a teardrop. Pinch the base to create a hat shape. Place the brim of the "hat" on the nonstick board and roll out around the central node, using the nonstick modeling stick or smooth ceramic tool. Release the shape from the board and place it on an area of the board that has been lightly dusted with corn starch.

11 Place the small rose calyx cutter over the top and cut out the calyx (or use the template on page 171). Remove the shape from the cutter and then place it back on the board to roll and elongate each of the five sepals.

12 Pick up the calyx. Open up the center with the pointed end of the nonstick modeling stick or smooth ceramic tool. Rest the calyx against your index finger and create a central vein on each sepal, using the fine end of the dresden veining tool.

13 Pinch the tip of each sepal between your finger and thumb. Moisten the center with edible gum glue and thread it onto the back of the flower, positioning a sepal over a seam in the petals. Pinch the back of the calyx and work it between your finger and thumb to thin it slightly. Remove any excess length. Dust the calyx with a mixture of foliage green and vine green petal dusts.

Mark five petals on the surface of the bud (15).

BUDS

14 Bend a hook in the end of a 28-gauge white wire, using needle-nose pliers. Form a cone shape of pale coral gum paste. Moisten the hook and insert it into the broad end of the cone. Pinch the bud to secure it in place.

15 Use the plain-edge cutting wheel or X-acto knife to create five petals in the surface of the bud. Leave to dry.

Tape the stem with quarter-width florist tape (16).

16 Dust to match the petal color. Add a calyx as described for the flower (see Steps 10–13)—a slightly smaller calyx cutter is required here. Tape over each stem with quarter-width nile green florist tape.

LEAVES

17 Roll out some pale green gum paste not too thinly, leaving a thicker ridge for the wire. Cut out the leaf using either a pelargonium leaf cutter or the template on page 172 and the plain-edge cutting wheel or X-acto knife. Insert a 26- or 24-gauge white wire moistened with edible gum glue into the thick ridge to support most of the length of the leaf.

18 Place the leaf ridge side uppermost on the nonstick board and use the broad end of the dresden veining tool to pull out at intervals around the edge to create a serrated effect. Soften the edge with the ball tool and then place the leaf into a double-sided pelargonium leaf veiner to texture. Remove from the veiner and pinch down the central vein and the side veins to give the leaf a little more movement. Leave to dry supported by paper towel or crumpled aluminum foil. Tape over the stem with half-width nile green florist tape.

COLORING

19 Dust the leaves in layers lightly with forest green, then overdust heavily with foliage green and vine green.

20 Use a mixture of coral and ruby petal dusts to catch the very edges of the leaf and add some color to the raised veins on the back of the leaf, too.

21 Dilute some eggplant and ruby petal dusts with clear alcohol. Use a fine paintbrush to add detail markings to the leaf. Follow the scalloped edge of the leaf to echo the painted markings. Leave to dry and then overdust the markings with eggplant petal dust. Spray the leaves very lightly with edible glaze spray.

ASSEMBLY

22 Use quarter-width nile green florist tape to tape together groups of buds and flowers. The buds should be kept lower than the flower heads. Tape the groups onto a 22-gauge white wire, using half-width nile green florist tape. Add small leaves in pairs down the main stem. Use the larger foliage at the base of the stems. Dust the main stems with foliage green petal dust and gently catch them with a mixture of eggplant and ruby petal dusts.

Petal dust locater

Stamen
Sunflower yellow (tips)

Pistil
Coral and red

Petals
Red, coral, and ruby (edges)

Calyx
Foliage green and vine green

Stem
Foliage green, eggplant, and ruby

Leaves
Forest green, foliage green, and vine green

Leaves (edges)
Coral and ruby

Leaves (details)
Ruby and eggplant

Ginger Lily

The Kahili ginger lily (*Hedychium gardnerianum*) is native to tropical Asia and the Himalayas. There are many varieties of ginger lily; the flowers vary in size and may be white, cream, yellow, orange, coral, or pink.

SKILL LEVEL ❀ ❀

Materials

- 33-, 30-, 28-, 26- and 22-gauge white wires
- White and pale green gum paste
- Edible gum glue
- Coral, ruby, white, sunflower yellow, plum, vine green, foliage green, and eggplant petal dusts
- Clear alcohol
- White and nile green florist tape

Equipment

- Wire cutters or florist's scissors
- Dusting brushes
- Fine paintbrush
- Nonstick board
- Nonstick rolling pin
- Grooved board (optional)
- Simple leaf or heart-shaped cutters or templates on page 169
- X-acto knife
- Curved fine scissors
- Ceramic tool
- Double-sided stargazer B lily petal veiner
- Ceramic silk veining tool
- Foam pad
- Ball tool
- Plain-edge cutting wheel

PISTIL

1 Cut a length of 33-gauge white wire into thirds using wire cutters or florist's scissors. Take a tiny ball of well-kneaded white gum paste and blend it onto the wire about $1\frac{1}{2}$–2 inches (4–5 cm) from the tip.

2 Next, work the paste between your finger and thumb toward the end of the wire. Pinch off the excess paste as you work to create a nice, fine coating on the wire.

3 Use your finger and thumb to curve the length of the pistil gracefully.

4 Next, form a tiny sausage shape of white gum paste and work both ends into a slight point. Secure the sausage to the end of the wire using a tiny amount of edible gum glue. Leave to dry a little before coloring.

Paint the anther an intense red (5).

5 Dust the length of the pistil with coral petal dust. Dilute a small amount of ruby petal dust with clear alcohol and paint the sausage shape an intense red, using a fine paintbrush.

HEART-SHAPED PETAL

6 Roll out some well-kneaded white gum paste, leaving a thick ridge for the wire (a grooved board may be used for this). Cut out the petal shape using the larger simple leaf cutter, a heart-shaped cutter, or the petal template on page 169 and an X-acto knife. Insert a 28-gauge white wire moistened with edible gum glue into the thick ridge of the petal to support about half the length. Work the base of the petal down onto the wire to elongate the shape slightly.

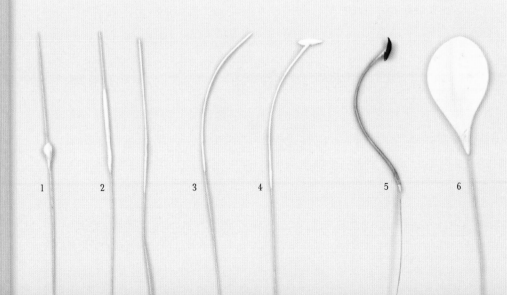

1   2   3   4   5   6

Cut a "V" using sharp scissors (7).

Curve the small side petal back slightly (9).

SIDE PETALS

10 Roll out some well-kneaded white gum paste, leaving a thick ridge for the wire (again, a grooved board may be used to speed up the process). Cut out a petal shape, using the smaller simple leaf cutter. Insert a 30-gauge white wire moistened with edible gum glue into the thick ridge of the petal to support one-third to half the length of the petal. Pinch the base of the petal onto the wire to slightly elongate it. Place the petal on the firm foam pad or the palm of your hand and soften the edge, using the ball tool.

11 Texture the petal using the stargazer B petal veiner, then remove it from the veiner and pinch gently from the base through to the tip to accentuate a central vein. Curve back the petal slightly. Repeat to make a second petal.

Work a piece of gum paste onto a 33-gauge wire (12).

OUTER PETALS

12 Take a length of 33-gauge white wire and cut it into shorter lengths using wire cutters or florist's scissors. Take a tiny piece of well-kneaded white gum paste and work it onto a wire to create a fine coating.

7 Use curved fine scissors to remove a "V"-shape cut from the top edge of the petal to create a heart-shaped petal. Place the petal ridge side up on the nonstick board and use the ceramic tool or nonstick rolling pin to broaden the top section of the petal slightly.

8 Place the petal in the double-sided stargazer B lily petal veiner and press the two sides of the veiner firmly

together to texture the petal. Remove the petal from the veiner and rest it against your index finger.

9 Use the ceramic silk veining tool to frill and texture the edge slightly. Next, using your finger and thumb, gently pinch the petal from the base through to the tip to accentuate a central vein. Curve the petal back slightly.

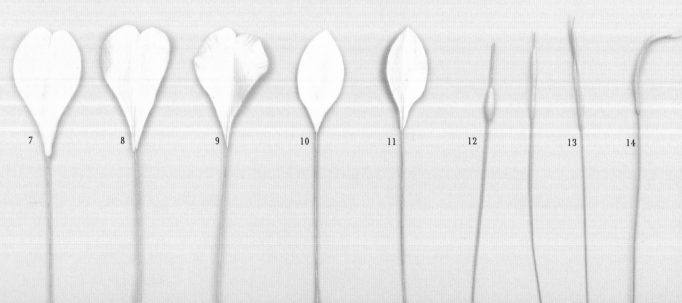

7   8   9   10   11   12   13   14

Shape the outer petals with your fingers and thumb (14).

ASSEMBLY AND COLORING

15 Mix together white petal dust with a touch of sunflower yellow petal dust. Dust each of the petals gently from the base through to the tip to create a soft coloring. Mix together coral, plum and white petal dusts to add a tinge of color to the base of each of the three petals, fading the color toward the center.

13 Place it on the nonstick board and use the flat side of the stargazer B petal veiner to flatten the petal shape, then place it in the veiner to texture it.

16 Use quarter-width white florist tape to tape the large heart onto the pistil. Next, position and tape the two smaller petals onto either side of the large petal. Finally, add the three fine petals—two underneath the pistil and one tucked behind the flower.

14 Pinch the petal from the base through to the tip to accentuate a central vein. Curve slightly. Repeat to make three petals.

After assembling the petals, add a piece of gum paste to the wire to create the neck (17).

NECK

17 Next, create a fine neck to the flower by adding and blending a piece of white gum paste behind the petals. Work the paste between your finger and thumb to create a slender neck. Pinch off any excess length. Curve the neck slightly. Dust with the light sunflower and white mixture from Step 15 to match the petals.

BRACT

18 Roll out some pale green gum paste thinly and cut out an arrowhead shape, using the plain-edge cutting wheel or X-acto knife. Soften the edge of the bract with the ball tool and then texture using the stargazer B petal veiner.

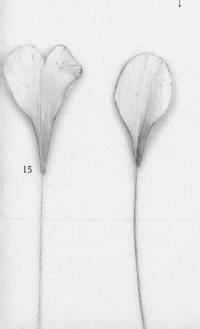

15

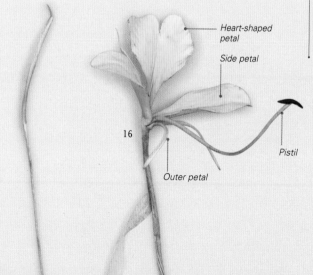

Heart-shaped petal

Side petal

Pistil

Outer petal

16

18

BUDS

21 Cut several lengths of 26-gauge white wire into thirds, using wire cutters or florist's scissors. Next, form a teardrop shape of white gum paste. Insert a wire into the broad end of the teardrop and then work the base of it down against the wire to create a slender neck.

Pinch the point of the bract to make it sharper (19).

19 Moisten the bract slightly with edible gum glue and wrap around the neck of the flower. Pinch the point of the shape into a sharper point.

20 Dust the bract in layers, starting with vine green and then gently overdust with foliage green. Tinge the edges of the bract with a mixture of ruby and eggplant petal dusts.

22 Use your finger and thumb to pinch three fine petals from the pointed end of the bud. Twist the petals around the bud to create a spiral formation. Repeat to make buds in graduating sizes.

Attach the bract to the bud with edible gum glue (23).

23 Dust to match the flowers and add a bract, as described in Steps 18–20.

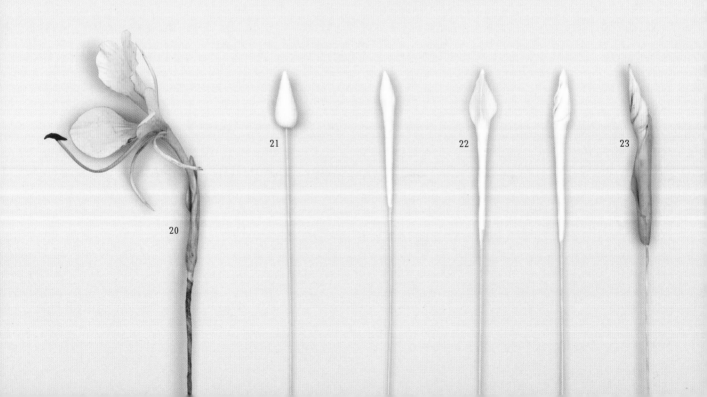

ASSEMBLY

24 Tape the buds onto a 22-gauge white wire, using half-width nile green florist tape, starting with the smallest and graduating in size. The buds are positioned all the way around the stem, although for sprays and arrangements it is often best to position them at the front of the stem.

25 Next, add the flowers. Dust the stem with vine green and foliage green petal dusts and a slight tinge of ruby and eggplant.

24

25

Petal dust locater

Anther head
Ruby

Pistil
Coral

Petals
White and sunflower yellow

Neck
White and sunflower yellow

Bract
Vine green and foliage green

Eggplant (edges)

Ruby (edges)

Hibiscus

There are seven species of hibiscus that are native to Hawaii. The flower pictured here is a large hybrid form that incorporates a wonderful clash of colors. Hibiscus vary in size and number of petals, with many being semi-double and double forms. The color range is vast, including white, pink, cerise, yellow, orange, red, and burgundy varieties.

SKILL LEVEL ❀ ❀ ❀

Materials

- 33-, 26-, 24-, and 22-gauge white wires
- Pale yellow and mid-green gum paste
- White and nile green florist tape
- Ruby, plum, sunflower yellow, tangerine, eggplant, foliage green, woodland green, and vine green petal dusts
- Clear alcohol
- Seed-head stamens
- Edible gum glue
- Pollen powder colored with sunflower yellow petal dust
- Half-confectionery glaze (see page 32) or edible glaze spray

Equipment

- Wire cutters or florist's scissors
- Needle-nose pliers
- Fine paintbrush
- Nonstick board
- Dusting brushes
- Nonstick rolling pin
- Large rose petal or hibiscus petal cutter or template on page 173
- Ball tool
- Foam pad
- Large hibiscus petal veiner
- Ceramic silk veining tool, cocktail stick, or short wooden skewer
- Paper ring former
- Dresden veining tool
- Angled tweezers
- Plain-edge cutting wheel or X-acto knife
- Double-sided hibiscus leaf veiner
- Hibiscus leaf cutters or templates on page 173
- Fine scissors (optional)

PISTIL

1 Cut five lengths of 33-gauge white wire, using wire cutters or florist's scissors. Use needle-nose pliers to bend a tiny hook in the end of each wire. Attach a tiny ball of pale yellow gum paste over the hooks. Leave to dry.

2 Tape the five pieces together using quarter-width white florist tape. Add a 26-gauge wire to give a little more strength and length.

3 Dilute some ruby and plum petal dusts with clear alcohol and paint the five sections of the pistil using a fine paintbrush. Leave to dry.

4 Wrap a ball of well-kneaded pale yellow gum paste around the length of the pistil, just below the five red sections.

5 Pinch the paste tightly at the top and work it down the length of the wire to create a long, slender platform. It should measure about the length of the petal you are making, although sometimes it can be longer. The base of the pistil is often slightly broader. Pinch off any excess paste. Smooth it between your palms or against the nonstick board. Give the length of the platform a gentle curve.

STAMENS

6 Cut lots of short lengths of small seed-head stamens. Insert them into the top section of the platform, just below the stamens. The exact number of stamens varies between varieties. Leave to dry a little before coloring.

7 Dust the upper section of the pistil and the stamens with sunflower yellow petal dust. Use plum to dust strongly from the base of the pistil. Next, paint the tips of the stamens with edible gum glue (or spray with edible glaze spray) and dip into the colored pollen powder to give the effect of pollen. Leave to dry.

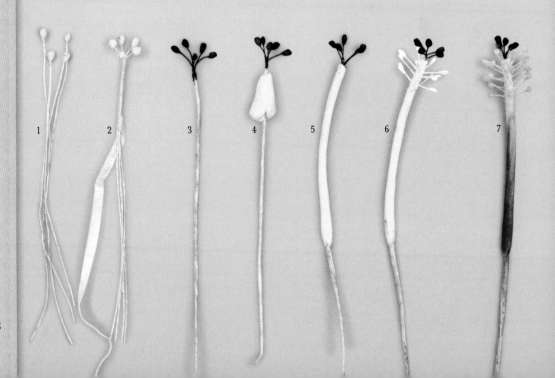

1   2   3   4   5   6   7

PETALS

8 Roll out some well-kneaded pale yellow gum paste, leaving a thick ridge for the wire. Cut out the petal using a large squashed rose petal cutter or large hibiscus petal cutter or the template on page 173 and an X-acto knife. Moisten the end of a 26- or 24-gauge white wire with edible gum glue (the gauge will depend on the size of flower you are making). Insert the wire into the thick ridge of the petal to support about half the length of the petal.

9 Soften the edge of the petal using the ball tool, working half on the edge of the paste and half on the firm foam pad or the palm of your hand.

10 Next, place the petal in the large double-sided hibiscus petal veiner and press the two sides together firmly to texture the petal.

Leave the petal to dry over a former (12).

11 Decide if you want to frill the edge—some varieties are frilly while others are not. Rest the petal edge against your index finger or against the nonstick board and use the ceramic silk veining tool, cocktail stick, or short wooden skewer to frill the edges gently.

12 Pinch the petal from the base through to the top edge to give a little shaping. Leave to firm up/dry a little over a curved paper ring former. Repeat to make five petals.

Add dark veining with a fine paintbrush (14).

COLORING

13 Dust the petals in layers, starting with sunflower yellow and then a touch of tangerine petal dusts. Keep the back of the petals much paler. Try to keep the area at the base of the petal free from coloring so that when you apply the plum petal dust to the base it keeps a fairly clean color.

14 Dilute some plum and eggplant petal dust with clear alcohol and add some dark veining at the base of each petal using a fine paintbrush.

Attach the petals to the pistil with florist tape (15).

15 Use half-width nile green florist tape to attach the five petals around the base of the pistil. It helps if the petals are still pliable at this stage, so that you can reshape them to give a more relaxed final flower.

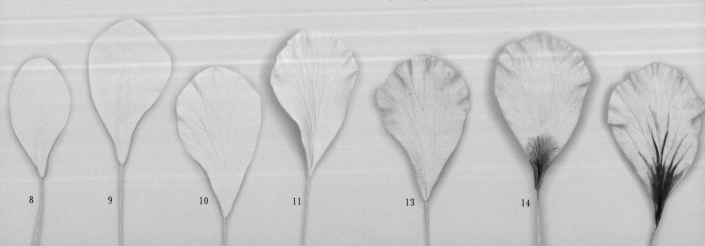

8 9 10 11 13 14

The first layer of sepals are attached with edible gum glue (17).

Shape the second layer of calyces with a curve backward (21).

The second layer of sepals is wired and taped to the base of the flower (22).

CALYX—FIRST LAYER

16 There are two layers of calyx at the back of the flower. The first layer consists of five sepals. Form a slender teardrop of well-kneaded mid-green gum paste.

17 Use the back or flat side of the large hibiscus petal veiner to press and flatten the shape, which will both increase its size and thin it out. Repeat to make five sepals.

18 Soften each sepal using the ball tool and then draw a central vein down each using the fine end of the dresden veining tool.

19 Attach a sepal to each of the five petals using a little edible gum glue. Position each sepal very close to the edge of each petal.

CALYX—SECOND LAYER

20 The second layer has between eight and 10 finer sepals. Cut 10 short lengths of 33-gauge wire, using wire cutters or florist's scissors. Attach a tiny ball of mid-green gum paste and work it onto the wire to form a fine, slender strand—the length varies between varieties.

21 Place on the nonstick board and flatten it. Pinch from the base through to the tip to give both a central vein and a curved shape. Repeat to make 10 sepals.

22 Tape the finer 10 sepals around the base of the first calyx, using half-width nile green florist tape. Dust both layers of the calyx with foliage green petal dust.

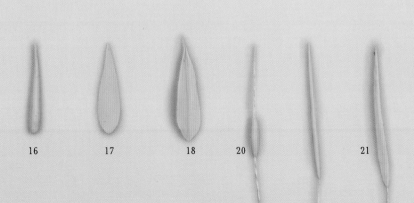

16   17   18   20   21

BUDS

23 Tape over a 22-gauge white wire with half-width nile green florist tape. Use needle-nose pliers to bend a hook in the end of the wire. Form a cone shape of pale yellow gum paste and insert the hooked wire into it to support quite a bit of the length. Pinch the paste at the base to secure it in place.

24 Use angled tweezers (without teeth) to pinch ridges into the sides of the bud to create five flanges/petals. Use your finger and thumb to pinch and thin the edges a little more.

Use angled tweezers to pinch five ridges into the surface of the bud to represent five petals (24).

25 Next, twist the petal in a clockwise movement to create a spiral effect.

26 Dust the bud with sunflower yellow petal dust. Add a calyx as for the flower (see steps 16–19).

LEAVES

27 Roll out some mid-green gum paste, leaving a thick ridge for the wire. Cut out the leaf using a hibiscus leaf cutter or hibiscus leaf veiner, or the template on page 173 and the plain-edge cutting wheel or X-acto knife. Insert a 26- or 24-gauge white wire into the thick ridge to support half the length of the leaf (the exact gauge will depend on the size of the leaf).

23   24   25   26   27   28

28 Place the leaf in a double-sided hibiscus leaf veiner and press firmly to texture. Remove the leaf from the veiner. If needed, use fine scissors to cut into the edge to give a more interesting serrated edge. You might also like to use the broad end of the dresden veining tool to thin the edges. Pinch the leaf from the base through to the tip to accentuate the central vein. Repeat to make leaves in varying sizes.

COLORING

29 The leaves can be a bright fresh green or very dark—this will depend on the variety of hibiscus and also on whether you are creating new growth or older foliage. Dust the leaves in layers with woodland green, foliage green and a little vine green petal dusts. Use a tinge of eggplant at the very edges.

30 Dip into a half-confectionery glaze or spray with edible glaze spray.

ASSEMBLY

31 Use half-width nile green florist tape to attach the leaves around the base of the bud and the flower. Increase the size of the leaves down the stem.

Petal dust locater

Pistil
Ruby (stamen heads)
Plum (stamen heads)
Sunflower yellow (upper section)
Plum (base)

Leaves
Woodland green, foliage green, and vine green

Plum and eggplant (base)

Eggplant (edges)

Petals
Sunflower yellow and tangerine

Calyx
Foliage green

29

30

Iris

SKILL LEVEL ❀ ❀

Materials

- Gum paste colored with deep purple petal dust
- 30-, 28-, 24-, and 22-gauge white wires
- Edible gum glue
- Deep purple, African violet, sunflower yellow, foliage green and white petal dusts
- Pollen powder colored with sunflower yellow petal dust
- Nile green florist tape

Equipment

- Nonstick board
- Nonstick rolling pin
- Miniature iris cutters or templates on page 170
- Wire cutters or florist's scissors
- Double-sided stargazer B petal veiner
- Dresden veining tool
- Dusting brushes
- Small ball tool
- Fine paintbrush
- Plain-edge cutting wheel
- Sharp scissors or tape shredder
- Foam pad

These fairly quick and effective miniature irises are based on the larger Dutch iris, although a lot of artistic license has been used to make this a simpler flower for the novice sugarcrafter. This size of flower is good to combine with other flowers in sprays.

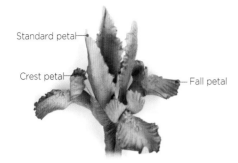

Standard petal

Crest petal — Fall petal

STANDARD PETALS

1 Roll out some gum paste colored with a little deep purple petal dust. Leave a slender ridge for the wire. These petals are quite narrow, so the ridge needs to be quite fine, too. Cut out a petal, using the slender cutter from the miniature iris set or the template on page 170 and an X-acto knife.

2 Cut a length of 30-gauge white wire into thirds, using wire cutters or florist's scissors. Moisten the end of a wire very slightly with edible gum glue. Insert the wire into the thick ridge to support about half the length of the petal.

3 Texture the petal using the double-sided stargazer B lily veiner. Next, work on the side edges of the petal with the broad end of the dresden veining tool to create a slightly tight frilled effect. Use the fine end of the tool to draw a central vein on the other side of the petal.

4 Pinch the petal from the base through to the tip to accentuate the central vein. Repeat the process to make two more petals.

FALL PETALS

5 Cut a length of 28-gauge white wire into thirds. Roll out some more pale deep purple colored gum paste, leaving a thick ridge for the wire. Cut out the petal using the fall petal cutter from the iris set or the template on page 170 and an X-acto knife.

6 Moisten the end of the wire with edible gum glue and insert it into the thick ridge to support about half the length of the petal.

7 Texture the petal using the double-sided stargazer B petal veiner.

8 Turn the petal over and draw a line down the center, using the fine end of the dresden veining tool. Pinch the petal from the base through to the tip to accentuate the central vein and at the same time create a ridge on the upper surface of the petal. Flick the edge a little to give more movement. Repeat to make two more petals.

CREST PETALS

9 Roll out more well-kneaded pale purple gum paste quite thinly. Cut out three crest petal shapes, using the crest petal cutters from the iris set or the template on page 170 and an X-acto knife.

10 Vein each petal using the double-sided Stargazer B petal veiner.

11 Use the broad end of the dresden veining tool to work, thin, and frill the two protrusions at the tip of the crest petals.

12 Pinch each petal down the center to create a ridge. Use the small ball tool to apply pressure behind the two protrusions to curl them back.

1 2 3 4 5 6 7 8 9 10 11 12

13   14   15   16

COLORING AND ASSEMBLY

13 Use a fine paintbrush to dust the standard petals with a mixture of deep purple and African violet petal dusts, fading the color toward the edges.

14 Use a fine paintbrush to paint a fine line of edible gum glue onto the ridge of the fall petal and dip the brush or ridge into some pollen powder colored with sunflower yellow petal dust.

15 Apply a little edible gum glue to the fall petals and attach the crest petals to them, ridge side up. Press the two together gently. Curl the two protrusions on each crest petal a little more if needed. Leave to firm up a little before coloring.

16 Dust the edges of the fall petals with the mixture of deep purple and African violet petal dusts. Use the same mixture to heavily color the top section and the edges of the crest petals.

Paint a fine line of edible gum glue onto the ridge of the fall petal (14).

Dip into pollen powder colored with sunflower yellow petal dust (14).

17 Tape the three slender standard petals together onto the end of a 22-gauge white wire, using half-width nile green florist tape.

18 Next, position and tape each of the fall/crest petal sections in between the gaps at the base of the standard petals, using half-width nile green florist tape.

BUDS

19 Tape over a 24-gauge white wire, using half-width nile green florist tape. Form a ball of pale deep purple gum paste into a cone shape. Moisten the hook of the wire with edible gum glue and insert it into the broad base of the cone. Work the base of the cone down onto the wire slightly to create a more slender neck shape.

20 Use the plain-edge cutting wheel to divide the surface into three sections. Pinch each section between your finger and thumb to thin them slightly and then spiral them around the bud. Dust as for the flower.

17   18

Divide the bud into three sections (20).

Twist the sections together (20).

BRACTS

21 These may be made with gum paste or, for a quicker and more flexible effect, use florist tape, as here. Cut lengths of about 1–1½ inches (2.5–4 cm) of half-width nile green florist tape.

22 Cut one end into a slender point.

23 Place the bracts on the firm foam pad or the palm of your hand and use the fine end of the dresden veining tool to draw a central vein down each one.

24 Attach the bracts in pairs down the stem. Dust with foliage green and white petal dusts mixed together.

ASSEMBLY

25 It is best to display irises in an upright position, just as they would grow in nature, as this shows off their wonderful fleur-de-lys shape. Here the buds and flowers have been simply grouped together and taped at the base, using half-width nile green florist tape.

Petal dust locater

Petals
Sunflower yellow (pollen powder)
African violet
Deep purple

Bracts
Foliage green and white

19 20 21 22 23 24

Easter Lily

Longiflorum lilies are usually white with yellow stamens, but there are now many hybridized forms, including this beautiful pink-tinged form with brown stamens. These highly scented plants are native to the Japanese Ryukyu Islands and to Taiwan, and are prized by florists and flower arrangers for large displays and also bridal work. They are often known as Easter lilies.

SKILL LEVEL ❀ ❀

Materials

- Pale green, white, and mid-green gum paste
- 33-, 26-, 24- and 20-gauge white wires
- Vine green, white, nutkin brown, terracotta, plum, daffodil, eggplant, woodland green, and foliage green petal dusts
- Confectioner's varnish (optional)
- Edible gum glue
- Nile green florist tape
- Three-quarter-confectionery glaze (see page 32) or edible glaze spray

Equipment

- Nonstick board
- Fine angled tweezers
- Plain-edge cutting wheel or X-acto knife
- Dusting brushes
- Wire cutters or florist's scissors
- Nonstick rolling pin
- *Longiflorum* lily cutters or templates on page 169
- Foam board
- Large ball tool
- Large double-sided *Longiflorum* lily petal veiner
- Dresden veining tool
- Needle-nose pliers
- Lily leaf veiner (optional)

PISTIL

1 Take a pea-size piece of well-kneaded pale green gum paste and insert a dry 26-gauge white wire into it. Use your finger and thumb to quickly work the paste down the wire, leaving a slightly bulbous tip. The length of the pistil can vary between varieties—here, it is about two-thirds the length of one of the petals. Pinch off any excess paste from the base of the pistil and then smooth it between your palms or against the nonstick board.

2 Next, flatten the bulbous tip slightly with your fingers and thumb and then use fine angled tweezers to pinch into three sections from the side of the pistil. Use the plain-edge cutting wheel or X-acto knife to divide the three sections from the upper surface of the pistil.

Pinch the top of the pistil into three sections using the fine angled tweezers (2).

3 Gently curve the pistil. Add a sausage of pale green gum paste at the base of the pistil to represent the ovary. Wrap it around and blend it into the main body of the pistil to form a slender oval shape. Use the plain-edge cutting wheel or X-acto knife to divide the ovary into six sections.

4 Dust gently with vine green petal dust mixed with a little white. The tip of the pistil is often very heavy with nectar—to create this effect, simply glaze the tip carefully with confectioner's varnish.

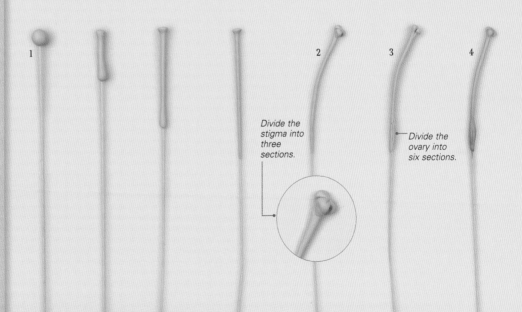

1   2   3   4

Divide the stigma into three sections.

Divide the ovary into six sections.

Score down the center of the anther (5).

STAMENS

5 Cut two lengths of 33-gauge white wire into thirds, using wire cutters or florist's scissors. Attach a very small piece of white gum paste to the end of a dry wire and blend it with your finger and thumb to form a sausage-shaped anther. Pinch off any excess length. Flatten the sides slightly and then mark a line down both sides of the anther using the plain-edge cutting wheel. Repeat to make six stamens.

6 Dust the length of the stamens with a mixture of vine green and white petal dusts. Color the anthers as required: here, they have been colored with a mixture of nutkin brown and terracotta petal dusts. Paint the anthers with edible gum glue and dip them into the petal dust mixture to create a pollen effect. Leave to dry. Use quarter-width nile green florist tape to tape the six stamens onto the pistil. Position them more toward one side, with their tips lower than the tip of the pistil. Tape them onto a 20-gauge white wire, using half-width nile green florist tape.

INNER PETALS

7 Roll out some well-kneaded white gum paste, leaving a long slender ridge for the wire. Use the broader of the two *Longiflorum* lily cutters or the template on page 169 and an X-acto knife to cut out a petal shape with the ridge running down the center of the petal.

8 Moisten the end of a 26-gauge white wire with edible gum glue and gradually feed the wire into the thick ridge so that the wire supports about half the length of the petal. Place the petal on the firm foam pad or the palm of your hand and use the large ball tool to soften the edge gently, but do not try to frill the petal.

9 Next, place the petal in a large double-sided longiflorum lily petal veiner, lining up the central vein markings of the veiner with the tip and the base of the petal. Press the two sides together firmly to give the petal texture.

10 Place the petal back on the firm foam pad and use the broad end of the dresden veining tool to work and hollow out the inner edges of the petal.

11 At this stage, it is best to apply any strong colors that you intend to use. Here, streaks of plum petal dust mixed with a little white have been added to the center of each petal.

12 Using half-width nile green florist tape, tape the three petals around the pistil/stamens. Space the petals evenly.

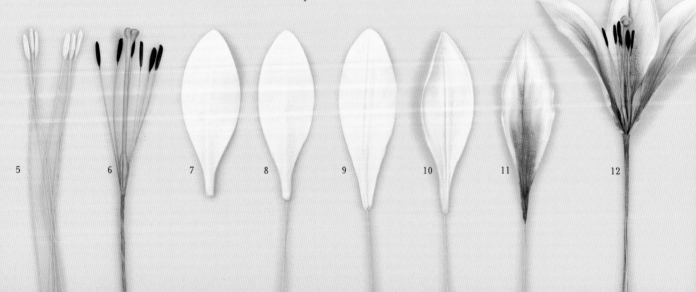

5   6   7   8   9   10   11   12

OUTER PETALS

13 Roll out some well-kneaded white gum paste, leaving a long slender ridge. Cut out three narrow outer petals using the narrow cutter from the *Longiflorum* lily set or the template on page 169 and an X-acto knife. Although these three petals are created using a thick ridge method, they are not wired. The central ridge simply gives the petals more support and strength.

14 Place the petal on the firm foam pad or the palm of your hand and use the large ball tool to soften the edge gently.

15 Texture the petal using the large double-sided *Longiflorum* lily petal veiner, lining up the central vein markings of the veiner with the tip and the base of the petal. Press the two sides together firmly.

Position the outer petals over the gaps left between the inner petals (17).

Press firmly togther (17).

16 Apply plum petal dust mixed with a little white down the center of the petal.

17 Moisten the lower half of each petal with a little edible gum glue and focus on the side edges rather than the middle of the petal. Position each petal on the back of the three inner petals, so that they cover the gaps left by the inner petals. Press the edges firmly onto the inner petals to secure them together. Curl the top sections of the petals back. At this stage, you will probably need to hang the flower to allow the petals to firm up a little. Re-curl as necessary.

18 Mix together vine green, daffodil and white petal dusts and add very pale tinges of color to the tips of each petal. Use plum and eggplant in layers on the back of the petals.

13   14   15   16   18

19 Once the flower has dried hold it over the steam from a just-boiled kettle to set the color and give a waxy finish (see page 32). Bend the stem at the base of the flower with needle-nose pliers to create a fairly acute angled position.

BUDS

20 Bend a hook in the end of a 20-gauge white wire, using needle-nose pliers. Take a large ball of well-kneaded white gum paste and form it into a cone shape. Moisten the hooked wire with edible gum glue and insert it into the broad end of the cone.

Score the bud to represent petals (22).

21 Work the broad base of the cone down the wire to create a long slender bud shape.

22 Use the plain-edge cutting wheel to create three sections to represent the outer petals. Use the tool to add finer central veining to each section.

23 Tape over the wire a few times with half-width nile green florist tape to create a fleshier stem. Color the bud to match the outer petals of the flower. Use needle-nose pliers to bend the wire at the base of the bud to angle the position of the bud.

LEAVES

24 Roll out some well-kneaded mid-green gum paste, leaving a long slender ridge for the wire. Use the plain-edge cutting wheel to cut a long, narrow leaf shape. Moisten the end of a 26- or 24-gauge white wire with edible gum glue (the gauge will depend on the size of the leaf). Insert the wire into the thick ridge of the leaf to support about half the length of the shape.

Bend the stem here.

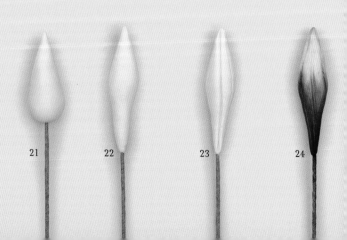

21   22   23   24

Here, veins have been added using a plain-edge cutting wheel (25).

Curve the leaf into shape with your fingers (25).

25 Texture the leaf using a double-sided lily leaf veiner or simply add a series of long veins using the plain-edge cutting wheel. Pinch the leaf from the base through to the tip to accentuate the central vein and also curve the leaf shape as you go. Repeat to make leaves in varying sizes.

COLORING

26 Dust the leaves in layers using woodland green and overdust with foliage green. Add a very light dusting of eggplant to the very edges of the leaves.

27 Spray the leaves with edible glaze spray or dip into a three-quarter-confectionery glaze to give a shiny finish.

ASSEMBLY

28 Tape the leaves onto the bud and flower stems using half-width nile green florist tape. Add extra 20-gauge wires to the stems as you work to give extra length and strength if needed.

25   26   27   28

Petal dust locater

Petals tips
Vine green, daffodil, and white mix

Petals center
Plum and white mix

Pistil
Vine green and white mix

Anther
Nutkin brown and terracotta mix

Petals back
Layers of plum and eggplant

Stamens
Vine green and white mix

Leaf edges
Eggplant

Leaves
Layers of woodland green and foliage green

Lisianthus

Also known as eustoma and prairie gentian, these pretty flowers are often used by florists for bridal work. *Eustoma grandiflorum* is a member of the gentian family, a native to the southern United States, Mexico, the Caribbean, and northern South America. The flower made here is a single variety—there are also double forms.

SKILL LEVEL ❀ ❀

Materials

- 33-, 28-, 26-, 24-, 22-, and 20-gauge white wires
- Pale green and white gum paste
- Edible gum glue
- Daffodil, vine green, white, foliage green, African violet, plum and eggplant petal dusts
- Nile green florist tape
- Quarter-confectionery glaze (see page 32) or edible glaze spray

Equipment

- Wire cutters or florist's scissors
- Smooth ceramic tool
- Nonstick board
- Foam pad
- Small ball tool
- Dusting brushes
- Needle-nose pliers
- Large rose petal cutter or template on page 172
- X-acto knife
- Ceramic silk veining tool
- Smooth angled tweezers
- Plain-edge cutting wheel
- Cattleya orchid wing petal or sage leaf cutter

PISTIL

1 Cut a length of 26-gauge white wire in half, using wire cutters or florist's scissors. Take a tiny amount of pale green gum paste and blend it onto the end of a dry wire.

2 Work the paste between your finger and thumb to create a fine coating. Pinch off any excess paste as you work.

3 Next, take a tiny ball of pale green gum paste and form it into a slight sausage shape.

4 Use the smooth ceramic tool to roll the central section of the sausage to thin it out slightly, creating a shape that resembles a figure-eight.

Hollow out the top of the pistil using the ball tool (6).

5 Flatten both sections of the shape against the nonstick board.

6 Place the shape on a firm foam pad or against the palm of your hand and hollow out both sections, using the small ball tool or the rounded end of the smooth ceramic tool.

7 Now pinch the shape at the center, which will give an almost heart-shaped profile.

8 Moisten the tip of the pistil with edible gum glue and attach the heart shape, pinching the base of it firmly onto the wired section. In a just-opened flower these two sections are clenched tightly together, opening up gradually and looking almost like a pair of lips. Leave to dry a little. Dust the top of the pistil with daffodil petal dust.

9 Next add a ball of pale green gum paste at the base of this section to represent the ovary. Form the ball into an oval shape.

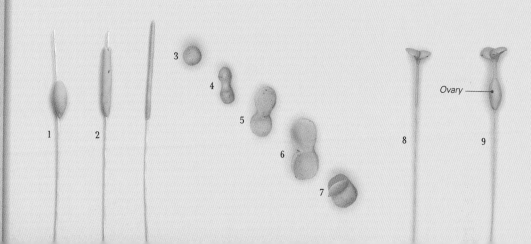

1 2 3 4 5 6 7 8 Ovary —— 9

STAMENS

10 Cut five short lengths of 33-gauge white wire, using wire cutters or florist's scissors. Use needle-nose pliers to bend the tip of each wire into a T-bar shape. Bend the end of the wire to a 90° angle and then hold this section halfway down and bend again to form a "T" shape. Attach a tiny amount of white gum paste over the top of the wire to create the anther. If the gum paste is soft enough, you won't need to use any edible gum glue to secure the paste to the wire. Repeat to make five stamens. Dust the T-bar with daffodil petal dust.

11 Use quarter-width nile green florist tape to tape the stamens around the pistil, positioning their tips lower than the tip of the pistil. Bend the length of the stamens to follow the curved line of the ovary. Tape the center onto a longer 22-gauge white wire to give support to the weight of the petals that will be attached.

12 Dust the length of the stamens and the ovary with a mixture of vine green, white, and foliage green petal dusts. Leave to dry.

PETALS

13 Use white gum paste or a pale version of the finished flower color to make the petals. Here, the gum paste has been colored with a tiny amount of vine green petal dust—this just takes away the harshness of white gum paste. Although the petals are unwired in this version of the flower, it is still advisable to leave a slightly thicker area at the base of each petal to give extra support to the final flower. Roll out some well-kneaded gum paste thinly, leaving a slightly thick ridge for the base of the petal. Cut out the petal using the large rose petal cutter or the large rose petal template on page 172 and the X-acto knife.

14 Pinch the thick base of the petal slightly to create a more slender shape.

15 Place the petal on the nonstick board and, using the ceramic silk veining tool, texture the surface of both sides of the petal. Use the tool at intervals across the petal, working very gently in a fan formation.

Use the ceramic silk veining tool to frill the petals (16).

16 Next, frill the top edge of the petal a little by resting the petal against your index finger and working the edge at intervals with the ceramic silk veining tool. Repeat the process to make five petals.

17 Moisten the base of the ovary/stamens with a little edible gum glue, turn it upside down, and attach the first petal onto the base of the stamens.

Curve to follow the shape of the ovary

10 11 12 13 14 15 16 17

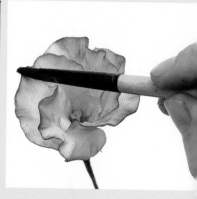

Curl back the edges of the petals (19).

Pinch and curl back the sepal (21).

21 Flatten the calyx slightly against the nonstick board and then pinch from the base to the tip. Repeat to make five sepals. Dust with a mixture of foliage green and white petal dusts.

COLORING AND ASSEMBLY

22 Mix together white, vine green, and daffodil petal dusts. Dust the base of each petal lightly to give a "glow" to the flower. Next, catch the edges of the petals with your chosen color—here, African violet and plum petal dusts were mixed together. Increase the color at the center of the top edge of each petal.

23 Tape the five sepals onto the base of the flower using quarter-width nile green florist tape.

Catch the edges of the petals with your chosen color of petal dust (22).

18 Next, moisten the base of the second petal and secure it on the left-hand side. Continue adding the petals to create an even spiral, tucking the last petal underneath the first petal.

19 Pinch the base of the petals firmly against the wire to create a tight bond and a slightly finer neck. Curl back the edges of the petals slightly. Hang the flower for a while to dry a little

and keep going back to check the shape and re-curl the edge if needed.

CALYX

20 The calyx may be made quickly with twisted florist tape or, if time permits, as follows: Cut five short lengths of 33-gauge white wire using wire cutters or florist's scissors. Take a small ball of pale green gum paste and work it onto the wire to form a fine strand.

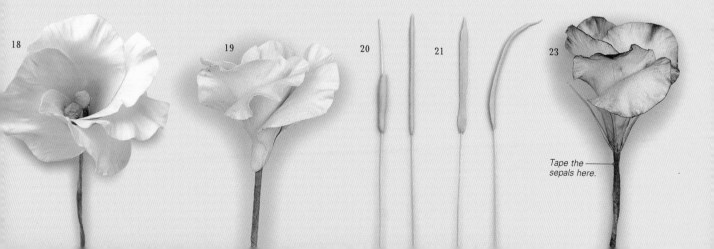

18
19
20
21
23

Tape the sepals here.

BUDS

24 The buds occur in pairs and vary in size. Form a cone of pale green gum paste. Bend a hook in the end of a 24-gauge white wire using needle-nose pliers, then moisten the hook with edible gum glue and insert it into the base of the cone to support quite a bit of the bud's length. Pinch the paste onto the wire at the base and work it between your finger and thumb to create a slender neck.

25 Use angled tweezers (without teeth) to pinch five flanges into the sides of the bud. Next, pinch each flange/petal to thin the edges. Twist the petals around the bud from left to right.

26 Dust the bud to match the flower. The smaller the bud, the less of the actual flower color it will have. Add a calyx as for the flower (see Step 20).

LEAVES

27 The leaves occur in pairs. Roll out some well-kneaded pale green gum paste, leaving a thick ridge for the wire. The leaves are actually quite fleshy. Cut out the leaf shape using either the plain-edge cutting wheel and freehand technique or a cattleya orchid wing petal or sage leaf cutter.

28 Insert a 28- or 26-gauge white wire moistened with edible gum glue into the ridge to support about half the length of the leaf. The exact gauge will depend on the size of the leaf. Soften the edge of the leaf using the ball tool.

Create veins using the plain-edge cutting wheel (29).

29 Gently use the plain-edge cutting wheel to create a central vein and a few fine side veins. Pinch the leaf from the base through to the tip to accentuate the central vein. Repeat to make leaves in pairs of graduating sizes.

24   25   26   27   28   29

COLORING

30 Dust the leaves lightly with foliage green and white petal dusts mixed together. Add a little more foliage green to the base and center of the leaf on the upper surface to add a little depth. Add a gentle tinge of eggplant mixed with African violet petal dusts to the edges here and there. Dip the leaves into a quarter-confectionery glaze or spray very lightly with edible glaze spray.

ASSEMBLY

31 Use half-width nile green florist tape to attach two buds onto the end of a 20-gauge wire. Attach two small leaves where the stems join the main stem. Continue adding buds and leaves as required. The flowers can be attached in pairs or as a bud and a flower, once again taping two larger leaves where their stems join the main stem. Dust the stems with the green petal-dust mixture used on the foliage. Curve the bud and flower stems gracefully.

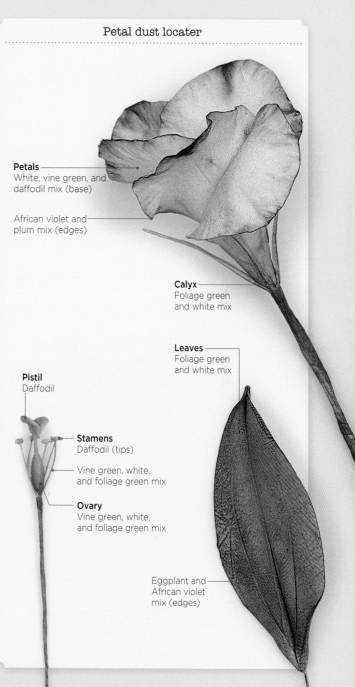

Petal dust locater

Petals
White, vine green, and daffodil mix (base)

African violet and plum mix (edges)

Calyx
Foliage green and white mix

Leaves
Foliage green and white mix

Pistil
Daffodil

Stamens
Daffodil (tips)

Vine green, white, and foliage green mix

Ovary
Vine green, white, and foliage green mix

Eggplant and African violet mix (edges)

30

31

Nasturtium

Nasturtiums (*Tropaeolum majus*) are often used as garden flowers and provide wonderfully cheerful color as well as a practical use, as the flowers, leaves, and fruit of the plant are edible, providing a wonderful peppery note to salads. They are actually quite an exotic plant, being native to Peru. The true wild form is orange, although there are many cultivated forms, providing a broad range of color. They are fascinating flowers to make, as many techniques are required to create the petals, calyx, bud, fruit, and foliage.

SKILL LEVEL ✿ ✿ ✿

Materials

- White stamens
- Hi-tack nontoxic craft glue
- 28-, 26- and 24-gauge white wires
- Sunflower yellow, tangerine, coral, ruby, eggplant, vine green, foliage green and white petal dusts
- Pale orange and pale green gum paste
- Edible gum glue
- Clear alcohol
- Nile green florist tape
- Full confectionery glaze, quarter-confectionery glaze (see page 32) or edible glaze spray

Equipment

- Fine scissors
- Nonstick board
- Nonstick rolling pin
- Nasturtium petal and calyx cutters or templates on page 170
- X-acto knife or plain-edge cutting wheel
- Ceramic silk veining tool
- Nonstick modeling tool or smooth ceramic tool
- Double-sided nasturtium petal veiner (or similar)
- Dresden veining tool
- Dusting brushes
- Fine paintbrush
- Fine angled tweezers
- Needle-nose pliers
- Five-petal blossom cutter
- Large stephanotis cutter
- Double-sided nasturtium leaf veiner
- Tea light

Secure the stamens to the end of the wire (1).

STAMENS AND PISTIL

1 Take four white stamens and line up their tips. Bend them in half to form eight tips. Add an extra stamen (with its tip cut off) to represent the pistil. Use a little hi-tack nontoxic craft glue to bond them all together at the base. Squeeze them together to create a strong bond. Leave to set a little and then trim off a little excess bulk from the base using fine scissors. Next, attach the stamens to the end of a 28-gauge white wire using a little more hi-tack glue. Leave to dry and then curl gently using fine scissors. Dust the tips with sunflower yellow petal dust.

PLAIN PETALS

2 There are two plain-edged petals with fine detail markings. Roll out some well-kneaded pale orange gum paste, leaving a thick ridge for the wire. Cut out the petal, using the plain-edge petal cutter from the nasturtium set (squashed to match the template on page 170) or the template and an X-acto knife or plain-edge cutting wheel. Moisten the end of one-third of a length of 28-gauge white wire with edible gum glue and insert it into the thick central ridge of the petal so that it supports about half the length of the petal.

3 Place the petal, ridge side up, on the nonstick board. Use the nonstick modeling tool or ceramic silk veining tool to roll out and broaden the top edge of the petal.

FRINGED PETALS

4 You will need to make three of the fringed petals. Roll out some more well-kneaded pale orange gum paste, leaving a thick ridge for the wire. Cut out a petal, using the cutter from the nasturtium set that looks rather like a miniature guitar or the template on page 170 and an X-acto knife. Insert a 28-gauge white wire moistened with edible gum glue into the petal, making sure that it goes into the main upper section of the petal too, as this can be quite a fragile petal if it is not given enough support.

5 Work the bottom fine section of the shape down the wire to thin it out quite a bit and also elongate it. Pinch off the excess from the base.

6 Next, place it in a double-sided nasturtium petal veiner and press firmly to texture the petal. Remove the petal from the veiner and then rest it against your index finger and frill the edge very gently at intervals using the ceramic silk veining tool.

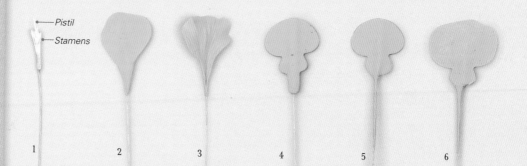

Pistil
Stamens

1   2   3   4   5   6

7 Place the petal on the nonstick board and work the small side sections at the middle of the petal using the broad end of the dresden veining tool, thinning them against the board.

8 Next, use fine sharp scissors to cut very fine slender "V"-shaped cuts into the two sections.

9 Pinch the petal from behind this section to push the fine cuts toward the surface of the petal. Repeat to make three fringed petals.

COLORING

10 Dust each of the petals using your chosen color. Here, the flower has been dusted using tangerine and coral petal dusts. The yellow flower was dusted with sunflower yellow and a touch of coral.

11 Add fine painted line markings to the two plain petals, using a fine paintbrush and some ruby and eggplant petal dusts diluted with clear alcohol. Add some shorter markings to each of the fringed petals (not all varieties have these lines). Leave the paintwork to dry and then add a touch of dry ruby and eggplant petal dusts mixed together to the center of the painted markings.

ASSEMBLY

12 It is best to assemble the flower while the petals are still a little pliable. Use quarter-width nile green florist tape to attach the two plain petals to the stamens, so that the stamens curve toward the petals. Next, add the three fringed petals to the opposite side of the flower. While the petals are still pliable, reshape and give a little more movement to the flower shape.

CALYX

13 Color some gum paste with sunflower petal dust and add a touch of pale green gum paste, too. Form a ball of paste into a long teardrop shape. Pinch out the broad end of the teardrop between your fingers and thumbs to create a witch's hat shape.

14 Place the brim of the hat on the nonstick board and use the nonstick modeling tool or smooth ceramic tool to roll out the brim of the hat to make it a little finer. Next, place the

nasturtium calyx cutter or the template on page 170 over the long section of the hat (this is the nectary), guiding one of the sepals of the five-sepaled cutter closer to the nectary, and cut out the shape. It will stick in the cutter, so rub your thumb over the paste against the cutter to create a good clean cut. Push the calyx out of the cutter using the nonstick modeling tool or smooth ceramic tool.

Add the three fringed petals second

Curve the stamens toward the plain petals

Add the two plain petals first

7   8   *Cut "V"s here.*   9   10   11   10   11   12

Open up the throat of the nectary (16).

Indent on either side of the nectary (18).

15 Place the calyx back on the nonstick board and imagine the calyx as a human figure, with a head, two arms, and two legs. Use the nonstick modeling tool or smooth ceramic tool to broaden the two arms. Broaden the other three sepals very slightly, too—but not as much as the arms.

16 Pick up the calyx and use the pointed end of the smooth ceramic tool to open up a hole leading through to the nectary. Use the fine end of the dresden veining tool to draw a central vein on the inside of each of the five sepals.

17 Moisten the center of the calyx with edible gum glue and thread the wired flower through the calyx just below the hole created for the nectary. Position the two plain petals so that the nectary sits behind them, with the "head" sepal covering the seam between them.

18 Use fine angled tweezers to pinch the nectary to create an indent on either side of it. Curve the length of the nectary a little. Allow to firm up before dusting with sunflower petal dust. Add a tinge of vine green petal dust mixed with foliage green to the tip of the nectary.

LARGE BUDS

19 Bend a hook in the end of a 24-gauge white wire using needle-nose pliers. Tape over the wire using half-width nile green florist tape. Form a ball of pale orange gum paste into a cone shape and pinch out the broad end to form a hat shape. Place it flat on the nonstick board and thin out the brim of the hat. Cut out the shape, using the five-petal blossom cutter or the template on page 170 and an X-acto knife.

20 Thin, vein, and frill the five petals using the ceramic silk veining tool.

21 Open up the center of the blossom using the pointed end of the nonstick modeling tool or smooth ceramic tool. Moisten the hooked wire with edible gum glue and thread it through the center of the blossom. Pinch the back of the blossom firmly around the work

and thin the back slightly between your finger and thumb. Pinch off any excess length. Moisten the petals slightly and squeeze them together to form the appearance of petals just emerging. Leave to dry.

22 Dust the bud to match the color of the flower.

23 Add a calyx as described for the flower (see steps 13–18), but use the large stephanotis cutter instead.

14

15
Head
Arms
Nectary
Legs

17

19

20

21

22

23

SMALL BUDS

24 Bend a hook in the end of a 28-gauge white wire, using needle-nose pliers. Tape over the length with quarter-width nile green florist tape. Form a tiny teardrop shape of pale green gum paste. Pinch the broad base and work it between you finger and thumb to create a slender nectary. Use an X-acto knife or plain-edge cutting wheel to divide the pointed end of the bud into five sections.

25 Moisten the hooked wire with edible gum glue and insert it into the underside of the bud. Pinch it to make it secure around the hook. Curl the nectary. Leave to dry, then dust lightly with vine green petal dust.

SEED PODS

26 Bend a hook in the end of a 24-gauge white wire. Tape over the length of the wire with quarter-width nile green florist tape. Roll a ball of well-kneaded pale green gum paste. Moisten the hooked end and insert it into the ball.

27 Use an X-acto knife or plain-edge cutting wheel to divide the seed pod into three sections.

28 Use fine angled tweezers to pinch a series of fine ridges down each section. Insert a short length of stamen thread into the center of the seed pod to represent the pistil leftover by the flower.

29 Dust the pod lightly with vine green petal dust. Mix together eggplant and ruby petal dusts and catch the ridges of the pod to highlight them. Leave to dry. Glaze using full confectionery glaze or spray with edible glaze spray. Use needle-nose pliers to create interesting curled stems.

LEAVES

30 Tape over a 26- or 24-gauge white wire with quarter-width nile green florist tape—the exact gauge will depend on the size of the leaf you are making. Use needle-nose pliers to bend a small loop in the end of the wire. Bend the wire to create a ski pole shape in the wire.

31 Take a ball of well-kneaded pale green gum paste and flatten it between your fingers and thumb leaving a raised "pimple" at the center. Roll out the paste around the pimple using the nonstick modeling tool. Place the paste pimple side down in a double-sided nasturtium leaf veiner. Press the two sides together firmly to texture the leaf. Remove the leaf from the veiner and trim around it, using scissors or the plain-edge cutting wheel. Place the leaf on your hand and soften the edge very gently, using the ball tool. Place the leaf back on the nonstick board with the back of the leaf uppermost.

32 Light a tea light and then heat the end of the hook in the naked flame until it is red-hot. Quickly embed the hot hook into the pimple. The heat will create a fairly strong bond. Leave the leaf to dry a little before dusting. Repeat to make leaves in varying sizes.

COLORING

33 Dust the edges of the leaves with a mixture of ruby and eggplant petal dusts. Use foliage green to dust the leaves from the center fading out toward the edges. Overdust with vine green petal dust. The backs of the leaves should be much paler. Dip the leaves into a quarter-confectionery glaze or spray very lightly with edible glaze spray.

24   25   26   27   28   29   30   31

Etch veins with an X-acto knife (34).

Create insect bites with a red-hot wire (35).

34 Nasturtium leaves mostly have pale white veins; these can be created by scribing/etching away the veins using an X-acto knife. Alternatively, the lines can be painted using a fine paintbrush and a mixture of white petal dust (with a touch of foliage green added) and clear alcohol.

INSECT NIBBLES

35 These are optional but quite fun to create. Heat a metal scriber or strong wire in the tea light flame until red-hot, then quickly pierce holes and nibbles in the edges of the leaves. The sugar will caramelize, leaving small holes with brown edges.

ASSEMBLY

36 Form trailing stems by taping leaves onto a 22-gauge wire, using half-width nile green florist tape. Start adding the small leaves, graduating the size as you work. Gradually introduce the small buds at the same point as a leaf. Alternate the position of the leaves and buds as you create the trailing stems. Eventually, add the flowers, again adding them at a connection between a leaf and the main stem.

32

33

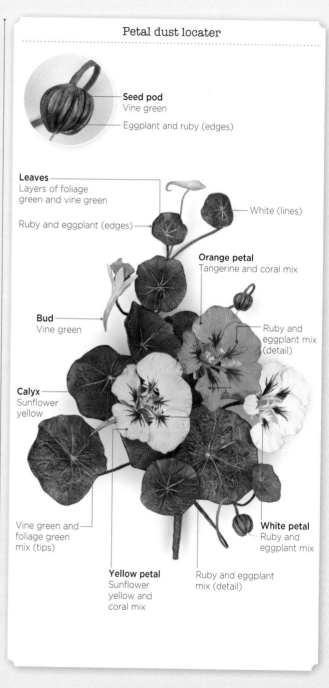

Petal dust locater

Seed pod
Vine green

Eggplant and ruby (edges)

Leaves
Layers of foliage green and vine green

Ruby and eggplant (edges)

White (lines)

Orange petal
Tangerine and coral mix

Bud
Vine green

Ruby and eggplant mix (detail)

Calyx
Sunflower yellow

Vine green and foliage green mix (tips)

Yellow petal
Sunflower yellow and coral mix

Ruby and eggplant mix (detail)

White petal
Ruby and eggplant mix

Passion Flower

The wonderfully exotic and ornate *Passiflora*. There are well over 500 species of passion flower. The variety pictured here is one of the larger varieties. This flower is very time-consuming to make, but very rewarding for the more adventurous sugarcrafter.

SKILL LEVEL ❀ ❀ ❀

Materials

- 35-, 33-, 26-, 24-, 22-, and 20-gauge white wires
- Pale vine green, white, and mid-green gum paste
- White and nile green florist tape
- Eggplant, vine green, white, sunflower yellow, deep purple, African violet, foliage green, woodland green, forest green, cream, and brown petal dusts
- Edible gum glue
- Clear alcohol
- Edible glaze spray
- Half-confectionery glaze (see page 32)

Equipment

- Wire cutters or florist's scissors
- Dusting brushes
- Nonstick board
- Plain-edge cutting wheel or X-acto knife
- Fine paintbrush
- Small nonstick rolling pin
- Large ruscus leaf cutter or narrow cattleya orchid sepal cutter or templates on page 171
- Foam pad
- Ball tool
- Double-sided stargazer B lily petal veiner
- Small rose petal cutter
- Dresden veining tool
- Briar rose leaf veiner
- Passion flower leaf cutters or templates on page 171
- Needle-nose pliers
- Paper towel or aluminum foil
- Tissue paper or cotton ball
- Sharp scissors

STIGMA

1 Use wire cutters or florist's scissors to cut three short lengths of 33-gauge white wire. Attach a tiny ball of pale vine green gum paste onto the end of one of the wires.

2 Use your finger and thumb to work the gum paste down the wire to create a slender neck, leaving a rounded bead shape at the tip. The length of these sections varies between varieties. Curve the length of the shape to form a relaxed "S" shape. Repeat to make three sections.

3 Use quarter-width white florist tape to tape them together tightly.

4 Dust the upper surface of each section with eggplant petal dust.

OVARY

5 Attach a ball of pale vine green gum paste just under the stigma and form it into an oval shape. The size of the ovary also varies between varieties. Dust the ovary with a mixture of vine green and white petal dusts.

Dust the upper surface of each section with eggplant petal dust. (4).

STAMENS

6 Cut five short lengths of 35- or 33-gauge white wires. Attach a tiny piece of well-kneaded white gum paste onto the end of the wire to create the short length of the filament.

7 Work the paste between your finger and thumb to make it very fine. Pinch off any excess length. Next, place it on the nonstick board and flatten slightly. Repeat to create five filaments. Curve the length of each slightly.

8 Now form the anthers: roll a tiny ball of white gum paste into a sausage shape. Moisten the tip of the filament with edible gum glue and press it into the center of the anther. Pinch the two together to create a secure connection. Use the plain-edge cutting wheel or X-acto knife to mark a line down the length of the anther. Repeat to add an anther to each of the filaments.

9 Leave to dry a little before coloring the anther with sunflower yellow petal dust and the filament lightly with a mixture of white and vine green. There are often tiny purple spots on the filaments, too, which can be painted on with a fine paintbrush using deep purple and African violet petal dusts diluted with clear alcohol.

10 Use quarter-width white florist tape to attach each of the stamens around the base of the ovary. Leave to dry. Tape an extra 26-gauge wire onto the main stem, using quarter-width white florist tape.

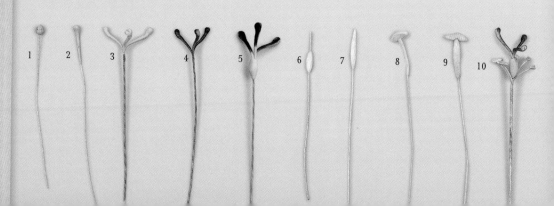

1   2   3   4   5   6   7   8   9   10

PLATFORM

11 Work a small amount of white gum paste just below the stamens down onto the wire to form a slender platform. This should be just less than 1 inch (2.5 cm) in length. Leave to dry. Next, attach a ball of white gum paste at the base of the platform. Pinch and form it into an almost curved triangular shape at the base. Use the plain-edge cutting wheel to mark a series of fine lines radiating to the edges of the shape. This represents the closed fine filaments around the base. Leave to dry.

12 The next step is optional. Roll out some more white gum paste thinly. Cut a long, very narrow strip using the plain-edge cutting wheel. Use the wheel to cut into one edge of the strip so that it resembles a fringe. Attach the fringe around the base of the platform, so that the fringe stands fractionally higher.

Attach and form a platform of white gum paste with your fingers (11).

OUTER FILAMENTS

13 You will need to make between 80 and 150 of these fine wired filaments! Cut several lengths of 35- or 33-gauge white wire into quarters, using wire cutters or florist's scissors. Attach a tiny ball of white gum paste to the wire and blend it toward the tip to create a very fine coating. The exact length of this will depend on the variety of passion flower you are making. Smooth the filament either against the nonstick board or between your palms. Repeat to make numerous filaments.

14 Create them in batches and tape them around the base of the platform while they are still slightly pliable, using quarter-width nile green florist tape. This will allow you to bend and reshape them as required. Some passion flowers have very straight filaments while others, like the flower pictured here, have more interesting shapes.

COLORING

15 Dilute some African violet and deep purple petal dusts with clear alcohol. Paint the ends of each of the filament with this purple mixture. Add tinges of the color to the tips of the narrow fringe around the base of the platform. Next, add eggplant petal dust to the mixture and add a band of color to form a ring around the center of the ring of filaments. Leave to dry. Steam or spray very lightly with edible glaze spray to set the color.

PETALS

16 Use the small nonstick rolling pin to roll out some very pale vine green gum paste, leaving a thick ridge for the wire. Use the large ruscus leaf cutter or narrow cattleya orchid sepal cutter to cut out the petal shape. Alternatively, use the template on page 171 and the plain-edge cutting wheel or X-acto knife.

17 Insert a 26-gauge white wire moistened with edible gum glue into the thick ridge to support about half the length of the petal. Place it on the firm foam pad or the palm of your palm and soften the edge using the ball tool, working half on the paste and half on the pad/palm.

18 Texture the petal using the double-sided stargazer B lily petal veiner. Remove it from the veiner and gently hollow the length using the ball tool. Pinch the petal from the base through to the tips. Repeat to make 10 petals. The flower pictured has 10 equal-sized petals, but, many varieties have five broad and five slightly narrower petals.

COLORING AND ASSEMBLY

19 Dust the 10 petals lightly with a mixture of vine green and white petal dusts. Catch the tips with African violet petal dust.

20 Use quarter-width nile green florist tape to secure five petals evenly spaced behind the stamens and filament center. Add the remaining five to sit in between the gaps.

Continue the lines of the petals on the base with the plain-edge cutting wheel (21).

21 Attach a ball of pale vine green gum paste behind the petals and flatten slightly. Use the plain-edge cutting wheel to continue the line of the petals onto the sides of the shape.

Pull at the edges of the bract with the dresden veining tool to create a serrated edge (22).

BRACTS

22 Roll out some mid-green gum paste and cut out three bract shapes using the small rose petal cutter or the template on page 171 and an X-acto knife. Use the broad end of the dresden veining tool to pull the edge at intervals to create a serrated effect.

23 Vein each bract using the briar rose leaf veiner.

Attach the bracts with edible gum glue (24).

24 Attach the three bracts to the base of the flower using edible gum glue. Leave to dry a little before dusting with a mixture of vine green, foliage green, and white petal dusts.

16   17   18   19   20   22   23

LEAVES

25 Use the small nonstick rolling pin to roll out some mid-green gum paste, leaving a thick ridge for the wire. Cut out the leaf using a passion flower leaf cutter or the leaf template on page 171 and the X-acto knife. Moisten the end of a 26- or 24-gauge wire with edible gum glue (the gauge will depend on the size of the leaf). Gradually insert the wire into the thick ridge to support most of the length of the central leaf section. Place the leaf on the firm foam pad and soften the edge with the ball tool.

26 Vein each section of the leaf in turn using the briar rose leaf veiner. Pinch the leaf down the center of each section to define the central veins. Pinch the tips a little and leave to dry on crumpled paper towel or aluminum foil. Repeat to make leaves in varying sizes.

LEAF COLORING

27 Dust the leaves in layers with woodland green, forest green, and foliage green petal dusts. Use foliage green and vine green on the smaller new-growth foliage. Catch the edges very gently with eggplant petal dust. Keep the back of the leaves lighter than the front.

28 Spray lightly with edible glaze spray or dip into a half-confectionery glaze. Leave to dry and then tape over each leaf stem with quarter-width nile green florist tape.

Curl the tendrils around a paintbrush handle (29).

TENDRILS

29 Use 35- or 33-gauge white wire to represent the tendrils. Dilute foliage green petal dust with clear alcohol and wipe the color onto the wire, using tissue paper or cotton ball. Leave to dry, then curl around a paintbrush handle or similar. Spray lightly with edible glaze spray to seal the color.

Draw a vein down the center of the florist-tape petal with the dresden veining tool (30).

FRUIT

30 Cut three small pointed petal shapes from a length of white florist tape, using sharp scissors. Use the fine end of the dresden veining tool to draw a series of veins down the length of each petal. Dust the petals with cream, white, and a touch of brown petal dusts.

25   26   27   28   30

31 Bend an open hook in the end of a 22-gauge white wire, using needle-nose pliers. Form a ball of well-kneaded pale vine green gum paste and insert the hook moistened with edible gum glue into the ball. Pinch the paste firmly around the base of the fruit to secure it in place. Gently apply a little pressure to the ball to form it into an almost egg shape. Pinch some of the paste down onto the wire to create a fleshier stem. Leave to dry.

32 Dust the fruit in layers with forest green, foliage green, and white petal dusts. Tinge with a little eggplant. Spray lightly with edible glaze spray. Tape the petals onto the base of the fruit using half-width nile green florist tape.

ASSEMBLY

33 Use a 24-gauge wire as a leading wire to start a trailing stem. Add a tendril at the end and tape using half-width nile green florist tape. Continue adding leaves, graduating in size down the stem. Add 22-gauge white wire and eventually 20-gauge wire as you work to create longer lengths to give more support. Add tendrils at leaf axils from time to time. Add the flower or fruit and a leaf at the same point.

Petal dust locater

Stamen filament
White and vine green mix

Stigma
Eggplant

Ovary
Vine green and white mix

Anther
Sunflower yellow

Platform
African violet and deep purple mix (center and edge)

Petals
Vine green and white mix

Filaments
African violet and deep purple mix (outer ring)

African violet, deep purple, and eggplant mix (inner ring)

Leaves
Layers of woodland green, forest green, and foliage green

Tendrils
Foliage green

Eggplant (edges)

Fruit
Layers of forest green, foliage green, and white Eggplant

Cream, white, and brown (petals)

Young leaves
Layers of forest green and foliage green

31   32

Rose

The ubiquitous rose! An essential for every cake decorator to master as it is the most popular flower used in cake decorating designs. There are so many varieties of rose—some are very neat in form and others have a more untidy appearance.

SKILL LEVEL ❀ ❀ ❀

Materials

- 30-, 28-, 26-, and 18-gauge white wires
- White, pale green, and mid-green gum paste
- Edible gum glue
- White vegetable fat
- Corn starch
- Nile green florist tape
- White, vine green, sunflower yellow, plum, African violet, eggplant, foliage green, forest green, and ruby petal dusts
- Half-confectionery glaze (see page 32) or edible glaze spray

Equipment

- Needle-nose pliers
- Nonstick board
- Paper towel
- Nonstick rolling pin
- Rose petal cutters or templates on pages 170 and 172
- Foam pad
- Metal ball tool
- Very large double-sided rose petal veiner
- Fine paintbrush
- Food-grade plastic bag or heavy plastic
- Smooth ceramic tool or short wooden skewer
- Paper towel ring formers or dimpled foam
- Dusting brushes
- Fine curved scissors
- Dresden veining tool
- Grooved board (optional)
- Rose leaf cutters or templates on page 170
- Large briar or tea rose leaf veiner

CONE CENTER

1 Bend a large open hook in the end of a half length of 18-gauge white wire using needle-nose pliers. Next, take a ball of well-kneaded white gum paste and form it into a cone. The length of the cone should measure about two-thirds of the length of the smallest rose petal cutter you are planning to use. Moisten the hook with edible gum glue and insert it into the rounded base of the cone so that it supports most of the length of the cone. Pinch the gum paste around the base using your finger and thumb to bond it to the wire. Reshape the point of the cone if needed. It is best to leave this cone center to dry overnight or for several days.

2 Color the gum paste as desired (see page 30). Although the flower pictured looks white, it has a touch of vine green food color added to the gum paste which gives a slightly warmer feel to a white or pale dusted rose. It is best to use a paler version of the final depth required.

FIRST LAYER

3 Grease the nonstick board with a small amount of white vegetable fat, then wipe it all off using dry paper towel. Using the nonstick rolling pin, roll out some well-kneaded gum paste very thinly on the nonstick board. Cut out four petals, using the smaller of the two rose petal cutters or the template on page 170 and an X-acto knife

4 Place each petal onto a firm foam pad or the palm of your hand and use the metal ball tool to soften the edge. Use the tool half on your pad/hand and half on the petal edge, using a rolling action with the tool. Do not frill the edge—you are only trying to thin it a little and take away the "cut" edge appearance.

5 Next, place each petal into the double-sided rose petal veiner and press firmly to texture the petal. It is not essential to vein the petals, but it does add interest and helps to create a more realistic effect. Remove the petal from the veiner and, using a fine paintbrush, moisten the base of the petal in a "V" shape with edible gum glue.

6 Position one petal against the dried cone (with the rounded edge at the tip) so that you have enough petal depth at the tip of the cone to allow you to create a tight spiral effect. It is important that the tip of the cone is not visible in the center of the flower. Do not worry at this stage about covering up the base of the cone.

7 Tuck the left-hand edge down and curl the petal around, leaving a little of the right-hand edge open so that you can tuck the next petal underneath it.

TIP
For roses that need to be made the same day, an alternative method of bonding the hook to the cone is to use a naked flame to heat the hook until it is red hot and then quickly and carefully insert the hook into the cone. The sugar will caramelize and set quite quickly, creating an instant bond.

1   3   4   5   6   7

SECOND LAYER

8 Start the second layer by tucking one of the three remaining petals underneath the first petal on the cone. Stick down the open edge of the first petal over the new petal from this second layer.

9 Place the next petal over the connection that has been created so that the connection is roughly at the center of the petal.

10 Turn the rose slightly around and tuck in the remaining petal. These three petals will form a spiral shape. Tighten two of the petals and leave the third petal edge slightly open, ready to receive the first petal of the next layer.

TIP
Some roses have slightly pinched petals—this can be done as you add each layer by pinching the top edges into a slight point with your finger and thumb.

Tuck petals underneath the preceding petal to cover the connections of the petals below (12).

ADDITIONAL LAYERS

The number of layers used will depend on how thin and tight you have made each layer and how much time you have. Sometimes it will take four layers, mostly five, and occasionally six. If you are short on time, then open the petals quickly so that you won't need as many layers.

11 Roll out more well-kneaded gum paste and cut out as many required sets of three petals using the same small cutter as before. Soften the edges of the next three petals and vein the petals using the large double-sided rose petal veiner. Cover the petals with a food-grade plastic bag or heavy plastic to stop them drying out.

12 Tuck the first petal underneath the open edge of the petal from the second layer, sticking/sealing down this petal over the top.

13 Again, add the next petal to cover the connection created.

14 The third petal tucks underneath the gap left behind to form yet another three-petal spiral.

TIP
It is important to keep positioning the petals over seams in the previous layer and not to line up the petals directly behind each other.

It is also important to keep each of the three petals at roughly the same height in each layer, increasing the height very slightly between each layer—but take care not to position them too high, as this creates a dark, sunken center.

15 Continue adding the remaining sets of three petals in the same way, gradually loosening the petals slightly to create a more open rose. Pinch the top edge of each petal as you add it and curl the edges slightly as you attach the final layer.

TIP
You can stop at any stage and add a calyx (see Steps 25–28) to create rosebuds of graduating sizes.

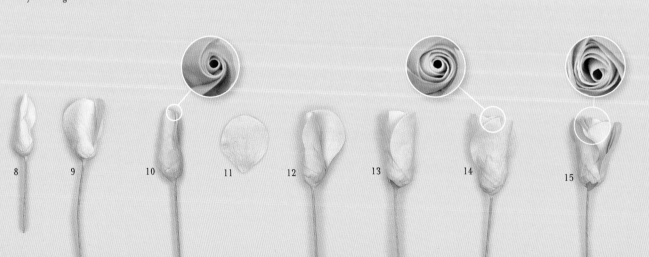

8   9   10   11   12   13   14   15

HALF ROSE

16 Roll out some more well-kneaded gum paste and cut out three petals, this time using the slightly larger rose petal cutter. Soften and vein the petals as before. Gently hollow out the center of each petal using the large ball tool or by simply rubbing the petal with your thumb.

17 Moisten the base of each petal with edible gum glue, painting a "V" shape again. Attach the first petal over a connection—this time the petals are not tucked underneath. Position the connection at the center of the petal. Pinch the base of the petal on either edge to retain the cupped shape and allow the rose to "breathe" a little.

18 Add the second petal next to the first so that it overlaps slightly and then add the third petal in the same way.

19 Use a short wooden skewer, paintbrush handle, or smooth ceramic tool—or even your finger and thumb—to curl back the side edges of each petal. At this stage you have created a "half rose." Slightly pinching the center of the top edge of each petal adds a little more interest and shape.

TIP
If the petals are not firm enough to support themselves, simply hang the flower upside down.

WIRED OUTER PETALS

You can continue adding the petals unwired directly to the half rose or, as illustrated here, you can wire each petal, giving the rose more movement and creating a less fragile finished flower.

20 Roll out some gum paste, leaving a subtle ridge down the center. Cut out the petal using the large rose petal cutter.

21 Bend a small hook in the end of a 26-gauge white wire (optional). Moisten the hook slightly with edible gum glue and insert it into the very base of the thick ridge. Pinch the base of the petal onto the wire to secure it in place. Soften the edges as before. Lightly dust the veiner with corn starch, then press the petal in the veiner firmly to create strong veins. Remove from the veiner and hollow out the center of the petal using your thumb.

22 Use the smooth ceramic tool, short wooden skewer, or your finger and thumb to curl back the two side edges. Leave the petal to dry slightly in a cupped shape: a paper towel ring former is good for this or you can use dimpled foam. Repeat to make eight to 10 petals—the number of petals varies with each rose. You may need to re-curl the petal edges slightly as they begin to firm up.

Tape the wired outer petals around the half rose (23).

23 Use half-width nile green florist tape to tape the wired outer petals around the half rose. It is best to do this while they are still slightly pliable in order to manipulate them to form a more realistic rose shape. Position the first petal over a connection and tape in tightly. Add the next wired petal over a connection on the opposite side of the flower. Continue adding the petals over connections and opposite each other until the desired effect has been achieved.

16

17

18

19

20

21

22

23

Here, plum, African violet, eggplant, and white petal dusts have been used to color the rose (24).

COLORING

24 If an intense coloring is required, the dusting can be applied as you build up the layers of the rose; however, this can be a messy process. For paler colors it is often best to assemble the rose first and then apply the color to the edges, as here. This flower has been dusted at the base of each petal with a mixture of white, a touch of vine green, and a touch of sunflower yellow petal dusts to help give a gentle "glow" from the base of the flower. The main color of the rose is a mixture of plum, African violet, eggplant, and white petal dusts. Concentrate the color at the center of the rose. Gently catch the edges of the outer petals.

CALYX

25 Cut five lengths of 30- or 28-gauge white wire. Work a ball of well-kneaded pale green gum paste onto the wire, forming a tapered carrot shape.

26 Use the flat side of one of the double-sided veiners to flatten the shape. If the shape is a little uneven, simply trim it with fine curved scissors.

27 Next, hollow out the length of the sepal using the metal ball tool. Pinch the sepal from the base through to the tip using your finger and thumb and then curve the tip back slightly.

28 Use fine curved scissors to create a few fine "hairs" into the edges of each sepal—the number of hairs varies between varieties, although generally one sepal has no cuts. Flick the hairs back slightly to open them up. If you wish, some of the "hairs" can be flattened using the broad end of the dresden veining tool.

Take care not to break the hairs of the sepal as you dust them (29).

29 Dust each sepal on the outer surface with a mixture of foliage green and a touch of forest green petal dusts. Add tinges of eggplant mixed with plum or ruby petal dust to the edges and tips of each sepal (this will depend on the variety you are making). Take care not to break the fine "hairs". Dust the inner part of each sepal using white petal dust, using the brush used for the green mixture on the outer surface. Lightly glaze or spray the outer surface only of each sepal, then set aside to dry.

ASSEMBLY

30 Use half-width nile green florist tape to tape the five wired sepals onto the back of the rose, positioning each sepal over a seam in the petals. Create an ovary/hip by adding a ball of pale green gum paste at the base of the sepals. Pinch, squeeze, and blend it into the base of the sepals to create a neat shape. Dust and glaze the ovary to match the sepals.

LEAVES

31 Rose leaves on commercial florist roses tend to grow in sets of three or five: one large, two medium, and two small. Roll out some mid-green gum paste, leaving a thick ridge for the wire (a grooved board may also be used for this job). Cut out a large leaf using the very large rose leaf cutter or the templates on page 170 and an X-acto knife. Remove the leaf from the cutter and then insert a moistened 26-gauge white wire into the thick ridge to support about half the length of the leaf.

25   26   27   28

30

32 Soften the edge of the leaf using the metal ball tool (do not frill) and then texture using the double-sided large briar or tea rose leaf veiner. Remove the leaf from the veiner and then pinch gently from the base of the leaf through to the tip to accentuate the central vein. Repeat to make two smaller leaves and two smaller sizes again. The gauge wire can be lighter the smaller the leaf gets (28- or 30-gauge).

COLORING

33 Dust the edges of each leaf so that they are heavier on one side/edge with a mixture of eggplant and plum or ruby petal dusts mixed together. Use this color on the upper stem surface, too. Dust the upper surface of each leaf in layers from the base fading to the edges with forest green and then heavier with foliage green and a touch of vine green. Dust the back of each leaf with white petal dust, using the same brush as for the green dusts. Spray lightly with edible glaze spray or glaze with half-confectionery glaze.

ASSEMBLY

34 Tape each of the leaf stems with quarter-width nile green florist tape and then tape into a set of five, starting with the large leaf and two medium leaves on either side followed by the two smaller leaves.

Front   *Reverse*

31   32   33   34

Petal dust locater

Leaves
Eggplant and plum or ruby mix (edges and upper surface)

White (back)

Layers of forest green, foliage green, and vine green

Petals
White, vine green, and sunflower yellow mix (base)

Plum, African violet, eggplant, and white mix (tips)

Calyx and ovary
Eggplant, plum, and ruby mix (edges)

White (inside)

Foliage green and forest green mix

Botany 101

Botanical terms are used throughout the book. If you are unsure of the difference between a stamen and a stigma, refer to the diagram here.

Templates

If you don't have the specific cutters required, use these templates to create the flowers in the book. See page 24 for instructions on how to use the templates.

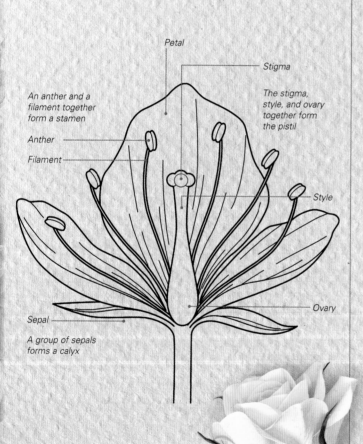

Petal

Stigma

An anther and a filament together form a stamen

The stigma, style, and ovary together form the pistil

Anther

Filament

Style

Ovary

Sepal

A group of sepals forms a calyx

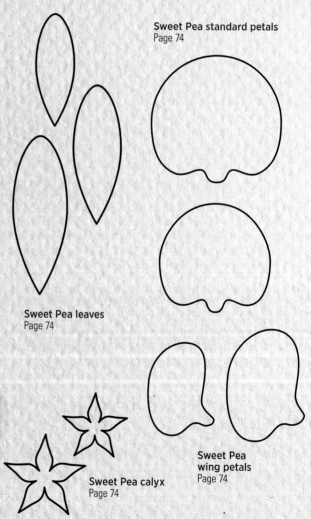

Sweet Pea standard petals
Page 74

Sweet Pea leaves
Page 74

Sweet Pea wing petals
Page 74

Sweet Pea calyx
Page 74

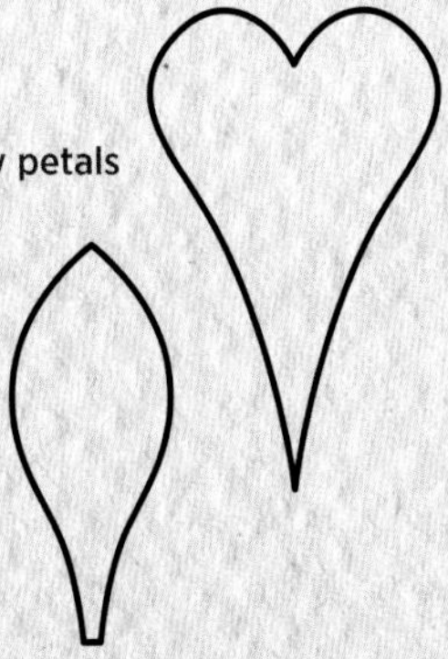

Ginger Lily petals
Page 122

Thistle leaf
Page 70

Babies' Bonnet
Page 80

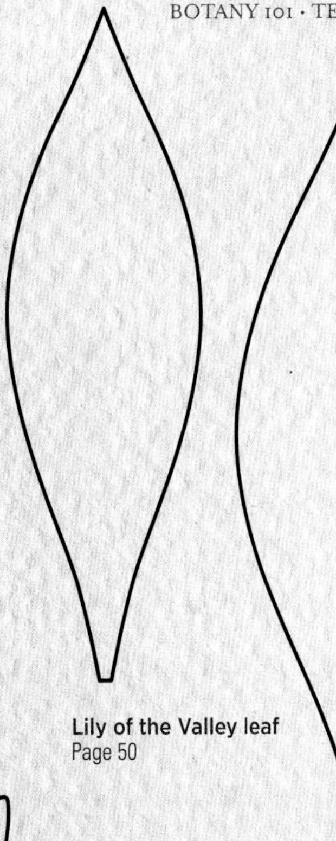

Lily of the Valley leaf
Page 50

Opium Poppy leaf
Page 88

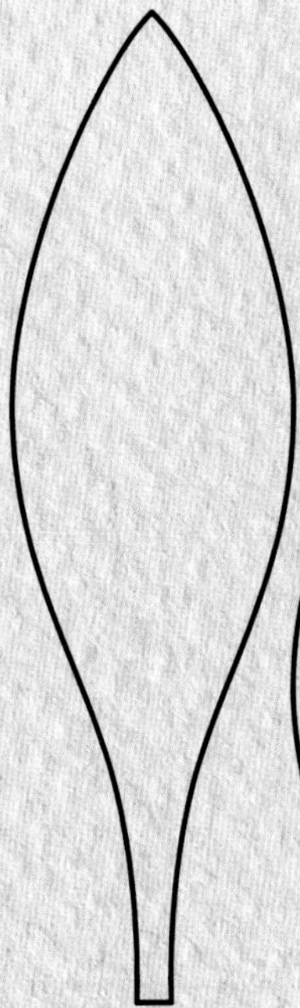

**Easter Lily
outer petal**
Page 138

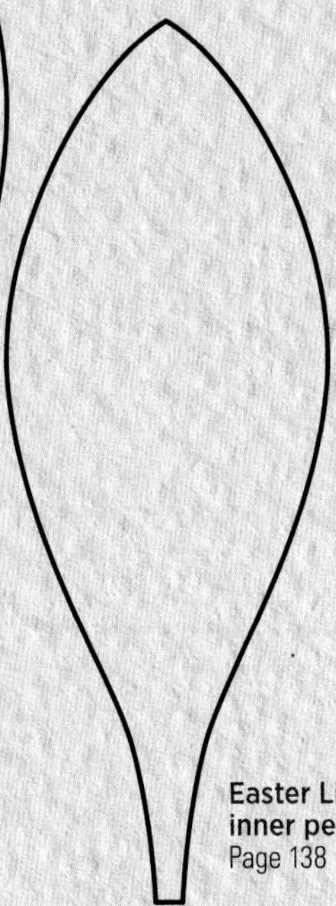

**Easter Lily
inner petal**
Page 138

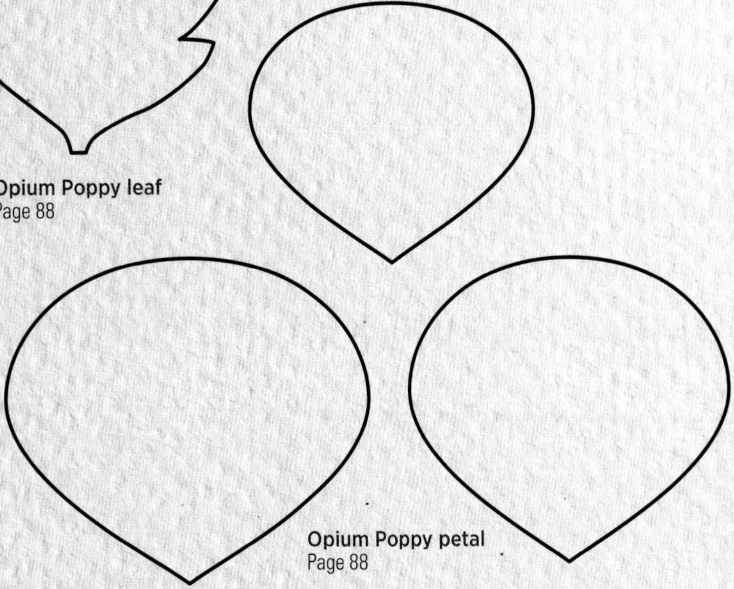

Opium Poppy petal
Page 88

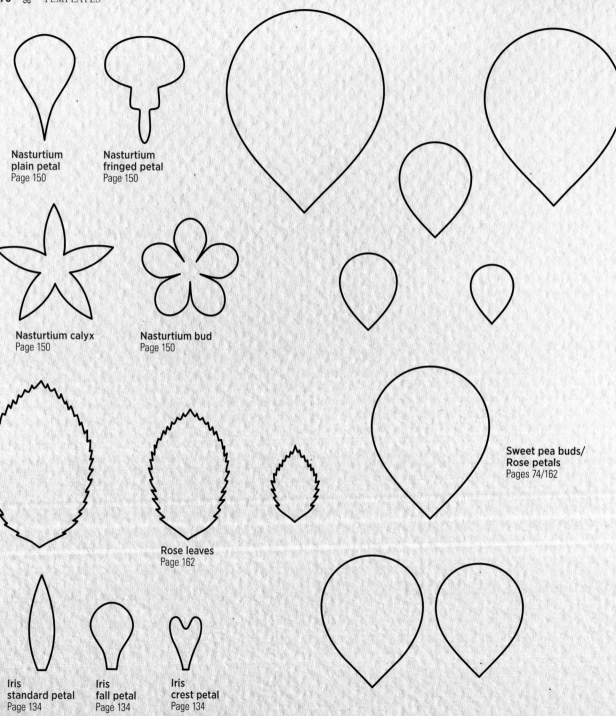

Nasturtium
plain petal
Page 150

Nasturtium
fringed petal
Page 150

Nasturtium calyx
Page 150

Nasturtium bud
Page 150

Rose leaves
Page 162

Sweet pea buds/
Rose petals
Pages 74/162

Iris
standard petal
Page 134

Iris
fall petal
Page 134

Iris
crest petal
Page 134

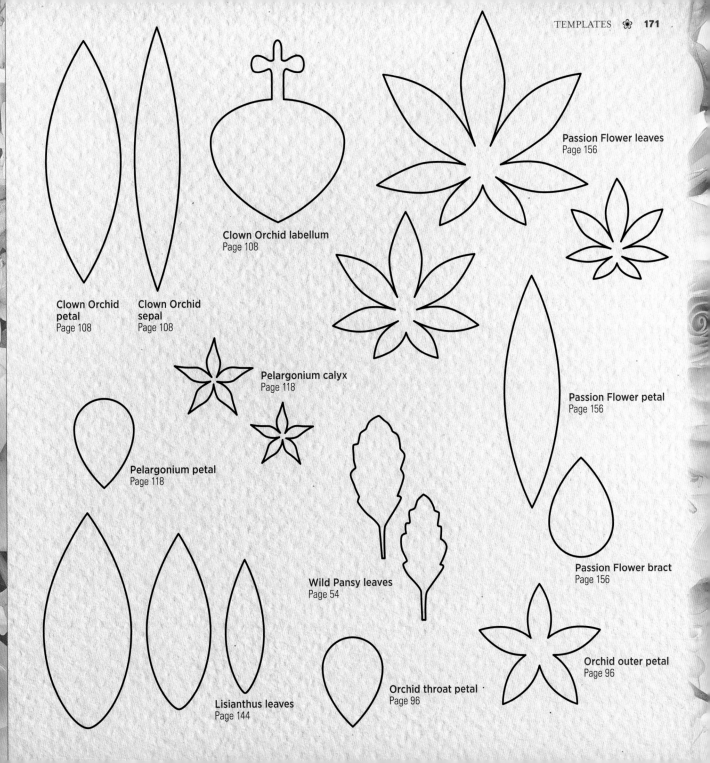

Clown Orchid labellum
Page 108

Passion Flower leaves
Page 156

Clown Orchid petal
Page 108

Clown Orchid sepal
Page 108

Pelargonium calyx
Page 118

Passion Flower petal
Page 156

Pelargonium petal
Page 118

Wild Pansy leaves
Page 54

Passion Flower bract
Page 156

Lisianthus leaves
Page 144

Orchid throat petal
Page 96

Orchid outer petal
Page 96

Anemone petal
Page 100

Pelargonium leaves
Page 118

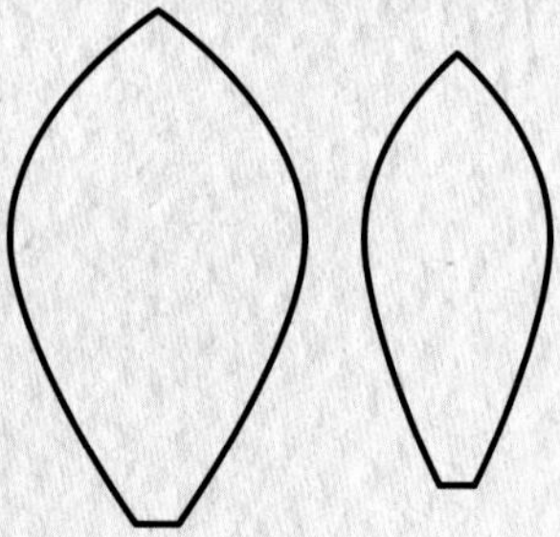

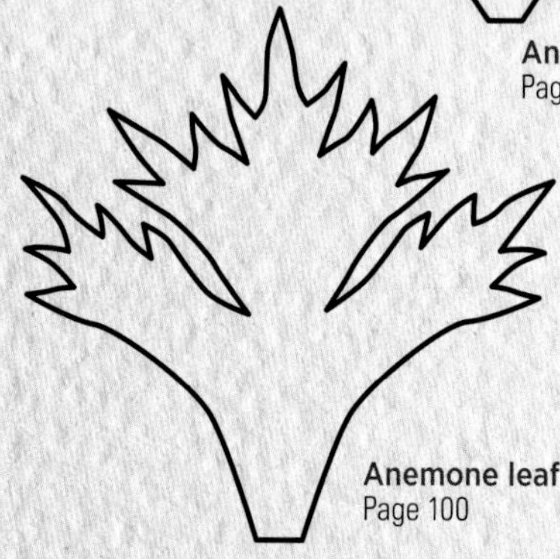

Anemone leaf
Page 100

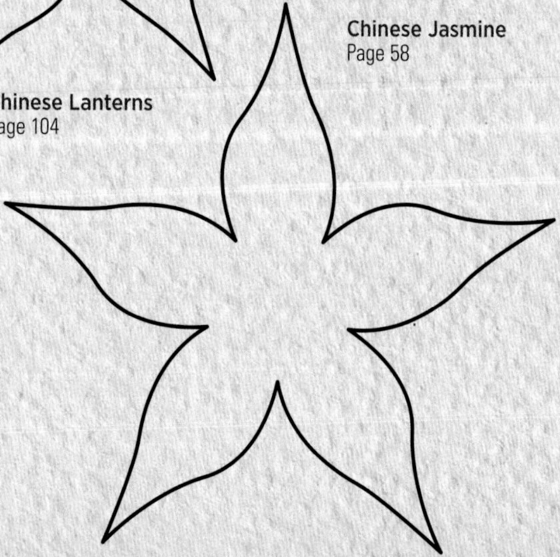

Chinese Jasmine
Page 58

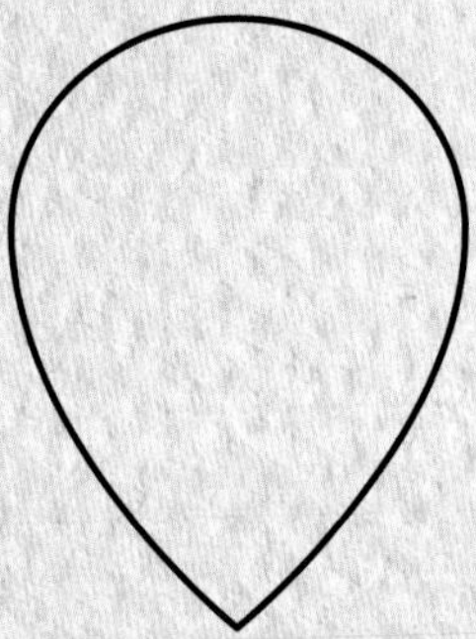

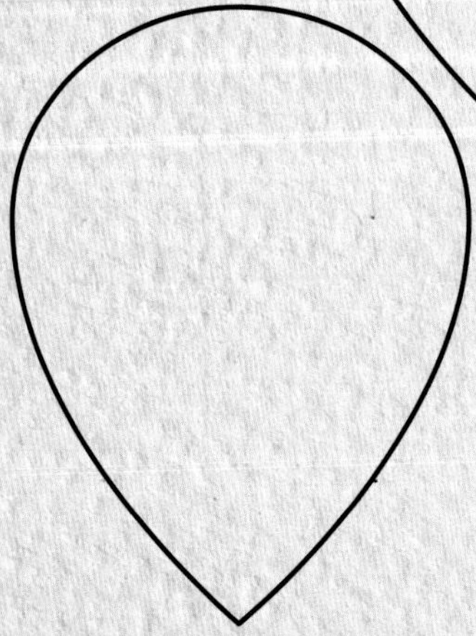

Chinese Lanterns
Page 104

**Peony/Lisianthus/
Large Rose petals**
Pages 66/144/162

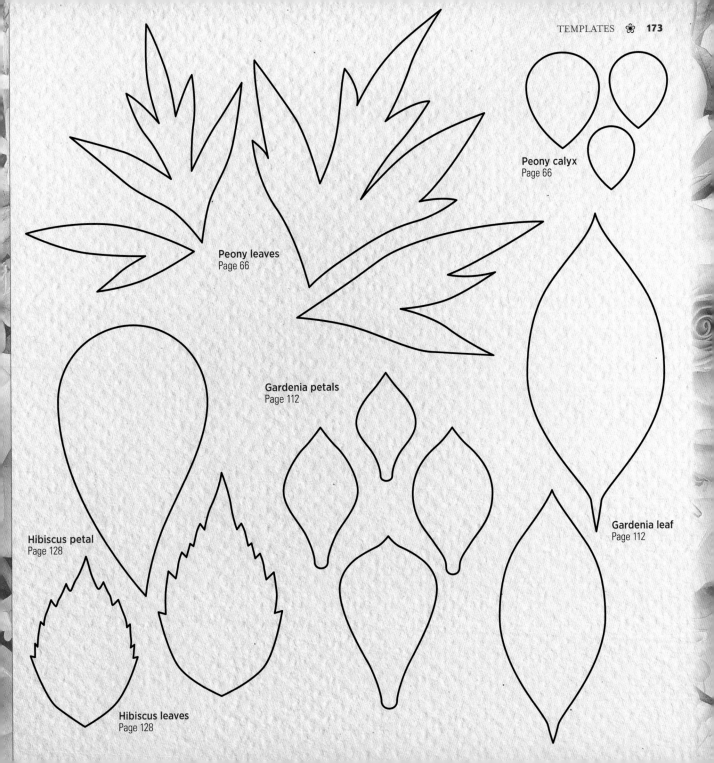

Peony calyx
Page 66

Peony leaves
Page 66

Gardenia petals
Page 112

Gardenia leaf
Page 112

Hibiscus petal
Page 128

Hibiscus leaves
Page 128

Index

Credits and suppliers

All step-by-step and other images are the copyright of Quarto Publishing plc. While every effort has been made to credit contributors, Quarto would like to apologize should there have been any omissions or errors—and would be pleased to make the appropriate correction for future editions of the book.

DEDICATION

A huge thank you to the following for their help and support during the writing and production of this book: Sathyavathi Narayanswamy, Alice Christie, Tombi Peck, Andrew Lockey, Norma Laver, Jenny Walker, Beverley Dutton, Allen and Avril Dunn, John Quai Hoi and Roux and Liz. Also to the team at Quarto publishing who worked on this book: Victoria Lyle, Kate Kirby, Emma Clayton, Moira Clinch, Corrine Masciocchi, Philip Wilkins, and Penny Dawes.

CREDITS

Many thanks to the following companies who supplied mterials used in the book, particularly Squires Kitchen, who provided numerous pieces of equipment for the Essential skills chapter:

SQUIRES KITCHEN
www.squires-shop.com
Tel.: +44 (0) 1252 260260

A PIECE OF CAKE
www.sugaricing.com
Tel.: +44 (0) 1844 213428

ALDAVAL VEINERS
aldavalveiners@o2.co.uk
Tel.: +44 (0) 1670 790995

CELCAKES AND CELCRAFTS
www.celcrafts.co.uk
Tel.: +44 (0) 1759 371447

ELLEN'S CREATIVE CAKES
www.elenscreativecakes.nl
Tel.: +31 (0) 592 559202

FLOWER VEINERS
www.flowerveiners.nl
Tel.: +31 (0) 207 070446

MY CAKE DELIGHTS
www.mycakedelights.com
Tel.: 1-757-227-5351

THE OLD BAKERY
www.oldbakery.co.uk
Tel.: +44 (0) 1823 451205

THE SUGAR ART
www.thesugarart.com
Tel.: 1-817-297-2240

SUPPLIERS

A selection of recommended cake-decorating suppliers:

A.C. MOORE
www.acmoore.com
Tel.: 1-888-226-6673

BAKERY CRAFTS
www.bakerycrafts.com
Tel.: 1-800-543-1673

BULK BARN
www.bulkbarn.ca
Tel.: 1-905-886-6756

GOLDA'S KITCHEN
www.goldaskitchen.com
Tel.: 1-866-465-3299

GLOBAL SUGAR ART
www.globalsugarart.com
Tel.: 1-800-420-6088

HOBBY LOBBY
www.hobbylobby.com
Tel.: 1-800-888-0321

JO-ANN
www.joann.com
Tel.: 1-888-739-4120

KITCHEN KRAFTS
www.kitchenkrafts.com
Tel.: 1-800-776-0575

MCCALL'S
www.mccalls.ca
Tel.: 1-416-231-8040

MICHAELS
www.michaels.com
Tel.: 1-800-642-4235

WILTON
www.wilton.com
Tel.: 1-800-794-5866

CONTACT THE AUTHOR
www.alandunnsugarcraft.com